CONTENTS

GW00497862

FOREWORD

INTRODUCTION

1 EXTENDING A WARM WELCOME 8

2 MAKING THE MOST OF LIFE EVENTS 26

3 USING BUILDINGS CREATIVELY 44

4 CARING FOR GOD'S ACRE 62

5 BEING THE HEARTBEAT OF THE COMMUNITY 80

6 CELEBRATING OUR HERITAGE 96

7 CULTIVATING FRUITFUL FESTIVALS 110

8 WELCOMING MORE CHILDREN 128

9 REACHING THE ISOLATED AND LONELY 146

10 COMMUNICATING EFFECTIVELY 164

AFTERWORD 186

FOREWORD

BY HUGH DENNIS

If I am honest, I probably find it as surprising as you do that I have been asked to write the foreword to a book about rural churches. It isn't my normal line of country but let me give you a little context.

When I did the calculation, I discovered that for nearly half my life I have lived next door to churches of various shapes and sizes.

Admittedly I have no memory of the first one, the Parish Church of Kettering in Northamptonshire, but I feel certain that I must have been inside it, because my father was the curate, and I was born in the Rectory next door. I arrived in great haste apparently, shortly after lunch and masquerading as indigestion, and there was no time to get to the hospital.

Next on my travels was Christ Church, on the Isle of Dogs, in the East End of London, where in 1962 when I was a mere three months old, my father became the rather cool, pipe-smoking vicar.

A decade later, we were off again, to Mill Hill in North London and a parish in which Robert Atwell, the author of the introduction to this book, now Bishop of Exeter, was my father's curate. This was followed by stints in Yorkshire, where my father, now a suffragan Bishop, served in the Diocese of Ripon, and then in Suffolk as Bishop of St Edmundsbury and Ipswich.

Even on holiday we liked to be next door to churches, and most of my summer holidays were spent in rural parishes around England where my father borrowed the vicarage as a base, in return for taking the services while the usual vicar was away.

You might think, quite reasonably, that a childhood of such proximity to churches would mean that I would step away from the habit in adult life, but not a bit of it. Instead, I bought a house next to a small church in the South Downs, one of eight churches in a team parish in the Diocese of Chichester.

In other words, when it comes to churches and parishes, I am something of an insider with a particular love for rural churches, and a great sympathy for those who toil to keep them going in what are often very difficult circumstances.

Stand on the top of any hill in the English Countryside, look down onto the patchwork of trees and fields beneath, and almost certainly somewhere in that landscape you will see the spire or tower of a place of worship, dominating the skyline of the village in which they are set. They are often hundreds of years old, they have seen generation after generation enter through their hefty oak doors and have witnessed innumerable changes to the land that surrounds them, but it is the relatively recent past that has perhaps been most difficult for them, as agriculture has altered, employment opportunities have reduced, and the rural population has drifted to the towns.

Yet it would be folly to make the mistake of thinking that these buildings are simply historic monuments, facing inevitable decline. In my experience, they are often well loved, well used buildings that stand at the centre of the communities they serve, with halls and facilities that could be used, or indeed are already used, to bring the community together, be they churchgoers or non-churchgoers. During the pandemic, for example, many such churches have led the way in organising networks of support. The same pandemic, in one of its rather unexpected consequences, has changed the outlook for rural areas as, helped by the move to homeworking, families increasingly look to leave larger towns and cities to experience the peace and quiet of the countryside.

So, if anything, I think many rural churches are rather like spring bulbs, ready for the right conditions to release all the potential they hold, and to thrive. Some are already growing and blossoming, and many others will follow.

And that is why I am delighted to be writing the foreword to this book, dedicated as it is to the flourishing of the rural church. The real authors of the book are the many thousands of people nationwide who love and care for their village church. By reading about just a few of their experiences, and drawing on the wisdom of ten eminent and experienced contributors, I hope that it will inspire you and help you identify simple ideas to involve people of all ages in building a welcoming, long lasting and thriving church community.

HUGH DENNIS
2022

ABOUT THE AUTHORS

INTRODUCTION
The Rt Revd Robert Atwell is the Bishop of Exeter and is the Lead Bishop for Rural Affairs in the Church of England and chair of the Liturgical Commission.

EXTENDING A WARM WELCOME
This chapter was developed by members of the Growing the Rural Church Project (**growingtheruralchurch.org**) of the Diocese of Exeter, led by **Sarah Cracknell** and **Katharine Otley**. The project was set up in 2017 to re-imagine mission in rural communities.

MAKING THE MOST OF LIFE EVENTS
The Revd Canon Dr Sandra Millar was Head of Life Events in the national Church of England for nine years with previous experience as a parish priest in Oxfordshire and as Children's Adviser in the Diocese of Gloucester.

USING BUILDINGS CREATIVELY
Marian Carson is Director of Operations at the Churches Conservation Trust (**visitchurches.org.uk**). She was previously Project Manager of the Diocese of Exeter's Growing the Rural Church project.

CARING FOR GOD'S ACRE
Harriet Carty is Director of Caring for God's Acre, a national charity which promotes the conservation of burial sites and supporting the volunteers who help to maintain them. Harriet has worked in conservation herself for over 30 years.

BEING THE HEARTBEAT OF THE COMMUNITY
Mark Betson is one of the National Public Policy Advisors for the Church of England supporting rural issues having a voice in both Church, government and wider society. He has also previously worked as an Environmental Scientist, a Vicar in the Diocese of Chichester and as a Regional Director for a farming charity.

CELEBRATING OUR HERITAGE

Geoffrey Hunter has been Head of Church Buildings and Pastoral in the Diocese of Ely since 2016, previously working in a similar role for the Diocese of London. He served as a churchwarden in his rural Norfolk parish until 2019 and has been a member of the Norfolk Churches Trust since a teenager. Geoffrey has sat on the Church Buildings Council since 2012.

Wendy Coombey, MBE, is Community Partnership and Funding Officer in the Diocese of Hereford She is also an elected member of the Church Buildings Council and a regular speaker at national conferences.

CULTIVATING FRUITFUL FESTIVALS

Helen Bent is a Worship Consultant and Trainer working with Praxis and a priest in a rural benefice. She was previously Head of Ministerial Training with the RSCM and has national involvement with GROW, the Group for Renewal of Worship and Leading Your Church into Growth.

WELCOMING MORE CHILDREN

Gill Ambrose is Chair for Godly Play UK (**godlyplay.uk**) and in her local community serves as a lay church minister and a school governor. She first trained and worked as a teacher and was also Children's Adviser for the Diocese of Ely for several years.

REACHING THE ISOLATED AND LONELY

Alison Selwood is an Executive PA at the Arthur Rank Centre, an ecumenical national charity, which resources, trains, and advocates for rural Christians, rural churches and the communities they serve. Together with colleagues, the Revd Elizabeth Clark and Fiona Fidgin, they have been pioneering work on rural isolation and loneliness.

COMMUNICATING EFFECTIVELY

Nick Edmonds is Deputy Head of News in the national Church of England office. He was formerly in the Diocese of Guildford for six years where he was Deputy Diocesan Secretary and Director of Communications. He is also a PCC member in a rural Hampshire parish.

INTRODUCTION

BY ROBERT ATWELL

'Hold fast to the head which is Christ,
from whom the whole body, nourished and
held together by its ligaments and sinews,
grows with a growth that is from God.'
Colossians 2.19

In our concern that the church should flourish, it is tempting to put numerical growth at the centre of our agenda. However, as Paul suggests, growth is less a target to be attained than the fruit of our relationship with Jesus Christ. Which is why nothing is more important for the life of the church, whether in the city, in a coastal or market town, or in the depths of the countryside than for its members to go deeper into God in prayer. Grace transforms. It releases energy for mission. It encourages us to invite others into the adventure of discipleship.

For hundreds of years our village churches have been at the centre of their rural communities. The English countryside is peppered with their towers and steeples. To a generation ambivalent about organised religion and allergic to dogma, but which craves the ether of spirituality, these buildings exert a powerful pull. In the words of Gerard Manley Hopkins, they remind us that 'there lives the dearest freshness deep down things'. They embody in brick and stone the changelessness of God. It is why a significant percentage of the rural population continue to see the village church as their spiritual home and the venue of choice for important moments in the lives of their families, be it a marriage, the christening of a child, or the funeral of a devoted grandparent. Their choice will be shaped as much by tradition and sentiment as religious commitment, and sometimes the parish church is the only community building left. Whatever the reason, the impact of a village church on its locality can be significant.

In spite of the fact that a higher percentage of the population go to church in the countryside than in the city, village churches are often perceived as millstones around the necks of their go-ahead urban cousins, sucking in precious resources which some claim would be better spent elsewhere. Rural clergy and hard-working lay officers often despair when they are compared negatively with large urban or suburban congregations, with success equated to strong numerical growth. Here lies part of the problem: village congregations are invariably small. But a small church is not a failed large church, any more than a satsuma is a failed orange.

This Guide seeks to fly the flag of the rural church. There are wonderful examples of exciting and healthy churches to be celebrated. There is wisdom to be shared from different traditions and contexts. Wherever we minister, there are things we can learn from each other about growth and sustainability, not least in the wake of the COVID-19 pandemic.

COVID-19's arrival in England in 2020 threw up a host of challenges, not least for small, beleaguered rural congregations. In some places, the pandemic brought to a head questions of viability that had been simmering below the surface but which had been too hot to handle. But it also generated unexpected opportunities. It forged coalitions of goodwill across historic divides, not only between different denominations but also between neighbouring parishes that paid lip service to collaboration but declined to cooperate. People rediscovered the gift of the local. In spite of patchy connectivity in remoter parts of the countryside, the internet has permitted more people to work from home and invest in their village. This bodes well for the longer-term health of rural communities, including their churches.

We have discovered new ways of being church and of worshipping online. Parishioners who for reasons of infirmity or disability were unable to attend their church felt included in the life of their worshipping community. We connected with 'the fringe' in ways that we longed to do for years. These good things need to be built on. We must not squander what we have learnt and return to old patterns; our virtual church doors need to remain open.

HOW WE USE OUR BUILDINGS

Of the Church of England's 15,700 churches, over 9,000 of them are located in areas of the country that are defined by the Government as rural. Of these churches, 36% are listed as Grade 1, 34% as Grade 2*, and 21% as Grade 2. Only 9% of our church buildings are ungraded. This is a rich heritage, but an expensive one to maintain and well beyond the pocket of most village communities. The poet Philip Larkin described his parish church as 'a serious house on serious earth'. Architectural gems though many of our churches may be, one of the fundamental things that we have re-learnt during the pandemic is that 'church' is people, not buildings. Now is the time to review their use and viability.

We have to face the fact that some of our village churches are not flourishing. Tiny congregations in single figures with a rising age profile, financial pressure and anxiety about dwindling resources have led some to pull up the drawbridge, batten down the hatches and turn in on themselves. Some can no longer muster a full complement of lay officers and those officers that are in harness often feel overwhelmed. For some churches, survival has become the name of the game.

Bear Grylls, the celebrity survival instructor, advises those marooned in a jungle to concentrate on basics: water, food and shelter. In similar vein, this Guide seeks to help those in positions of leadership, whether ordained or lay, to focus their energy on ten basic things that can contribute to the revitalisation, recovery and renewal of their village church.

Although written from a predominantly Anglican perspective, it seeks to draw upon the experience of other denominations who have their own stories and struggles to share. Rural congregations are increasingly ecumenical. The closure of some chapels (be they Methodist, Baptist or United Reformed) or the fact that the nearest Roman Catholic church may be 25 miles away, has generated an unexpected bonus for the Church of England in swelling our modest congregations. The presence of Christians nurtured in other traditions is enriching the worship of parish churches and giving new meaning to Anglican comprehensiveness.

WHAT IS RURAL?

The Government currently defines rurality by measuring population density, calculated by taking the number of households in a 30km radius. It defines a settlement as rural if it has a population less than 10,000 people and a small school as one with less than 210 pupils. These definitions make many who live in the countryside laugh because it is so removed from their experience. It also reveals how slippery the word 'rural' is and alerts us to the danger of lumping all 'rural' churches together. One size does not fit all.

Village communities and their churches are much more diverse than city dwellers imagine. Some congregations like to describe themselves as rural, but in reality are suburban both in their proximity to a town and in their outlook. People can claim to live in a village, except the majority of the inhabitants are newcomers and the 'village' is a dormitory of commuters who bemoan the moment a local farmer drops manure at the bottom of their driveway. This is why many dioceses prefer to describe certain parishes as 'remote rural' or 'deep rural' to differentiate them from those nearer market towns or larger centres of population. Typically, in remote rural areas, the same families have tilled the land for generations and there are few B roads, let alone A roads.

Unsurprisingly, remote rural communities can spawn congregations that are resistant to change, whether in relation to the introduction of new-fangled services, or the legal and structural changes of 'pastoral reorganisation', which might involve parishes joining together, boundary changes, or new ministry teams forming. Most traditional villagers presume that they belong to the church even if they do not attend it. Home groups and discipleship courses sometimes founder, not for any theological reason, but because traditional villagers may not like going into one another's houses. They know one another's business only too well and value their privacy. A minister needs to find other ways of building Christian community.

Statistically, the rural population is older than the urban population, and this is reflected in the age profile of most village congregations and the fact that there is rarely a critical mass of children and volunteers to work with them. Drawing more and younger people into the orbit of the worshipping community and encouraging them to take responsibility for the life of the church and its building is a struggle that this Guide seeks to help with. The sad reality is that in some villages, the same people are doing all the jobs, both in the church and in the wider community, and end up exhausted. The good news is that many villagers love their parish church, even if they don't worship in it. Rural communities are more rooted than their urban counterparts and have a fierce attachment to their buildings, churchyards and burial plots. We need to capitalise upon such sentiment because the bottom line is: use your village church or lose it. We need to make our buildings fit for purpose in the 21st century and make them work for their communities. If we do not, then the village church will go the same way as the village shop, the pub, the post office and the village school.

LEADERSHIP

As in all walks of life, it is the quality of the leadership, whether lay or ordained, that makes the difference and will determine whether a church grows or declines. Unlike suburban congregations that may have a modest pool of capable people to draw upon, the talent pool in rural communities is likely to be small. Rural clergy have little choice but to work with some individuals who are not natural leaders. That said, the strength of rural communities lies in their capacity for self-generation. People do not expect to be entertained; so they make their own entertainment. They are not on anyone's political radar and do not expect handouts; so they look out for one another. Here the rural church has things to teach the urban church. How can we release a capacity for self-generation in those inner-city communities that have become disillusioned or weakened by a culture of dependency? What is the secret of the resilience of the rural church?

Part of the answer lies in their grit. They operate on a long time-frame and have a strong sense of place. In the face of poor harvests, farmers persevere, knowing that eventually things will improve. Rural congregations instinctively understand the virtue of the old monastic prayer 'for grace to persevere with joy'. The agricultural community has an innate entrepreneurial ability to adapt. The theory of evolution, developed by Charles Darwin, was not the survival of the fittest, as is often erroneously stated. The species that survives is the one that is the most adaptable. The same is true of communities and churches. If the village church is to thrive, then it too needs to adapt. We need to adapt to a changing rural landscape: politically, following our departure from the European Union and the end of the Common Agricultural Policy; locally, in engagement with the changing nature of village communities; pastorally and liturgically, in the kind of worship we offer; and strategically, in simplifying church governance.

These themes run through this Guide in its concern to foster a spirit of entrepreneurism and experiment.

If the church in rural England is to flourish, then we need to release individual congregations from feeling that they have to be everything and do everything. Working together across an area and working ecumenically has to be the way forward. Mission and ministry in the countryside works best when people cooperate rather than compete. We need to generate an energy to work in partnership and to do so in new and imaginative ways for the sake of the kingdom of God. That is what this Guide aims to help with, by providing a menu of eminently practical, do-able things for local people to dip into and try out in their contexts. It is designed to address some key areas where applying relatively small changes can make a big difference, amplifying the efforts that may well be happening already.

Our churches are holy places that speak of God's unchanging love. If they are to survive as the home of living, praying congregations they need to recover their role as hubs of community life. And if our congregations are to thrive, they need to recover their confidence in the transformative power of the Gospel to change hearts and lives.

"FOR I WAS A STRANGER
AND YOU WELCOMED ME..."
MATTHEW 25.35

1

EXTENDING A WARM WELCOME

THREE KEY THINGS YOU'LL LEARN IN THIS CHAPTER

> If you want to grow you may need to change.

> How to make your church as welcoming as your home.

> Why structuring your welcome around strangers to the church, rather than those who are already friends, is key.

INTRODUCTION

I t is easy to tell ourselves that church is welcoming. We smile when new people come, and make sure they have a coffee and biscuit after the service. But welcome is more than this. From the language we use in signage to the way we structure our service, creating a warm welcome should be weaved into every strand of church life.

Think about when you invite someone to your home who has never visited before. You make sure that they know where you live and where to park. You will have a quick clean before they arrive.

Once they arrive, you offer them a drink and perhaps something to eat. If they have a hot drink you try and make it exactly as they like it. You offer them a comfortable chair and when they ask to use the toilet, you ensure they know where it is. If they bring children you make sure you have toys.

You won't assume that they already know that your spouse is called Terry and your dog is Toby, or that there is a low beam as you enter the living room – you will explain all of this naturally.

You will do all of this because you want them to feel welcome, to have a lovely time and to come again. If you're really honest, you probably also want to ensure that when they talk about their visit, everything is positive and glowing!

This approach needs to be the same with churches. We need to make them irresistible places for people to spend their time. Your welcome significantly affects the likelihood of people returning (and bringing others with them). In short, the way you welcome people, or not, affects church growth. If you are frustrated that your church is not growing, you may need to change the way you do things. Change is not always easy, but the suggestions in this chapter will give you the confidence to extend a much wider, warmer welcome.

WHO ARE YOUR VISITORS?

Consider who your visitors are – both current and the yet-to-be-welcomed. Are they tourists on a day out? Walkers? Grave visitors? Members of the congregation? Families? Guests to weddings, funerals or baptisms? The local school children, teachers and parents? People looking for a place of peace or solitude? Elderly visitors? Or young children? Visitors with restricted mobility?

It may be that your visitors include all of the above. Try to keep their different needs in mind. Remember visiting a church can be intimidating and even quite stressful; some people worry that there are lots of restrictions and rules, and may consider church to only be for people who are "holier" than they are. A closed gate or an awkward front door is enough to put some people off all together. Some visitors may also think that attending church is old fashioned and only for the elderly; it is important that through your welcome, you show that the church is still alive, current, and that the Christian message is open to everyone.

LOOKING AT THE PRACTICALITIES

Parking, access and churchyard

You may have a huge car park, or none at all. What is important is that visitors can plan their visit and know what to expect. Make sure your website is clear about parking and accessibility. Consider whether the pathways are accessible for

Photo credit: © Katharine Otley

wheelchairs and prams, if they are uneven or slippery, if there are handrails and where the nearest easy access toilet and baby changing facilities are.

If your church has a graveyard plan, make this as obvious and accessible as possible. Consider introducing seating in your graveyard, or maybe some picnic rugs and cushions in the summer?

What do your signs say about you?

People will judge your church when they look at the condition of your signs and noticeboards. If the signs look scruffy with an out of date poster in them, people will assume that the church itself is uncared for and dated in its approach. When looking at signage, look at the condition and whether they need a clean or a lick of paint. Be vigilant about removing out of date posters.

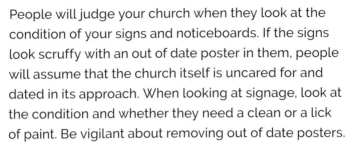

Look objectively at your noticeboards, or even better, invite someone else along who has never seen it and ask for their feedback.

As you look at your noticeboard your eye should be drawn to a large, warm message of WELCOME, encouraging people into church and putting them at ease. Whilst rotas, insurance certificates and so on may need to be displayed, there is no need to put them centre stage, maybe move them inside the church, or onto the website, (providing those who need it have access to it).

Remember that the welcome in the porch can make the difference between people walking in or walking away. Some may be nervous and will need encouragement to open the door. If your door is difficult to open then leave out some instructions so they don't think it's locked. If you have a service starting, have the door open with a person to greet, smile and welcome people inside.

Amazing A boards

Putting an A board outside your porch is a great way of reassuring visitors that the church is open and they are welcome.

Don't let language be a barrier

Using words such as eucharist, liturgy, sacrament, episcopal, denomination and diocese is bewildering for some people. Churches have a reputation for being full of rules and things you can't do, so try and keep your signs and language as plain, positive and inviting as possible. Avoid formal language and be as warm and conversational as you can.

Plasters, punctures and pups

If you have a lot of walkers or cyclists visiting your church, think about how the welcome to them could be made warmer. As well as water and biscuits, you may be able to offer hot drink facilities. Consider providing a puncture repair kit, a basic first aid kit, plasters, dry socks, or an area to charge mobile phones and don't forget the dog bowl! Always make sure that it is clear that anyone can help themselves; these are gifts for all, not just for churchgoers.

Housekeeping inside the church

By clearing away any unnecessary clutter, your church will appear calmer. It also helps visitors focus on key information. Visitors are often interested in the building's history, so ensure that any information you have on this looks up to date and appealing.

Being down with the kids

Parents may find a visit to church extremely stressful. Many feel that their children need to be silent and prevented from touching anything. How can your church make them feel welcome? Is there a clearly marked area for children to play in? Are there toys and books for different ages? Do you have nappy changing facilities? Maybe put up a sign to reassure parents that you are delighted to welcome children and fully expect them to be noisy. Try to ensure that there is a Sunday school offer for children and make this fun!

Cake and cushions

If you have volunteers who enjoy baking, consider offering some home baked cakes. This doesn't have to be every day; you could offer it during busy periods

or for a special event. Perhaps scatter some cushions around the church to give a more homely feel? Or have picnic rugs for people to sit on outside during the summer? A cupcake with the message "You are loved" piped on it might just change someone's whole perception of your church and give them confidence to return.

Online

Most people will look online before attending a church –
just like a restaurant, holiday or film – we research before
we commit. That is where the COVID-19 pandemic was
powerless to stop churches reaching people and it gave
people the opportunity to watch without having the
awkwardness of being watched. Make sure your website
screams 'welcome'. It should be clear when your services
are, how they can be accessed online (if you are offering
this); there should be pictures of friendly faces, and your
message to new people should be encouraging, loving
and relatable. Similarly to noticeboards, be mindful of the
language you use – keep it plain, positive and relevant to
new people as well as existing ones. There's more about
this in Chapter 10.

Photo credit: © Adam Shaw

HOW VILLAGE CHURCHES THRIVE

CASE STUDY

**A welcome in the Wolds – Weighton Wold Group,
East Yorkshire.**

This group of five parishes sits on the Yorkshire Wolds Way National trail. The Rector, the Revd Caroline Pinchbeck, says the numbers of people who simply visit the churches during the week, such as walkers and tourists, is around ten times the numbers attending Sunday services.

Caroline explained: *"Our spiritual heritage is the conversion of King Edwin of Northumberland in 627 AD by St Paulinus. There is much drama to the whole account which is told in our church windows.*

"We don't have the volunteers to sit in the church and tell this story in person, so we had to think of a way to offer welcome and hospitality to this 'silent congregation'. Some of them may well have questions about faith or are seeking connection with God, and we wanted to address that. Many people are inspired by the story of King Edwin and St Paulinus, and we use this as a springboard for helping visitors think about faith and spirituality today, and for sharing the Good News about Jesus."

If the church is closed, Caroline says there is a plastic box placed in the porch containing bottles of water, squash and biscuits. There is a Bible, some prayer cards with the 'pilgrimage window' explained and the prayer of St Paulinus. Information about local pubs and cafés, a map with suggested routes and some information about the other churches in the Group are also included.

When the churches are open, 'Top ten things to see while visiting our church' is displayed, along with prayer cards and history guides.

WHAT ABOUT FAITH?

———

"And how can they believe in him if they have never heard about him? And how can they hear unless someone tells them?"
ROMANS 10.14 (NLT)

Visitors to your church should not be able to leave your church building without being offered well-presented information about the Christian faith. The website Lifewords.global produces brilliant resources which are free and look really attractive. Consider having information for visitors who may be suffering with bereavement or mental health issues such as depression and anxiety. Ensure that the contact details for support services are somewhere obvious. Likewise, if there is an Alpha course or something similar running, make sure the details of this are up for people to see.

Welcome to this church

WE INVITE YOU TO USE THIS SPACE TO PRAY, REFLECT, MEDITATE OR SIMPLY HAVE SOME TIME OUT

PLEASE MAINTAIN PHYSICAL DISTANCING WHILE YOU ARE HERE AND BE CONSIDERATE OF OTHERS

HERE ARE SOME SIMPLE PRAYER IDEAS YOU MIGHT LIKE TO TRY

Look at one of the church windows. Is it plain or coloured? Does it tell a story? Can you see the light through it?

Spend some time gazing at the window and ask God to speak to you through it.

Use your fingers to pray:
Thumb - Give thanks for all the strong things in your life like relationships that sustain you.
Index finger - Say sorry for the times you've judged others or acted harshly.
Middle finger - Pray for all the important people who have power in the world.
Ring finger - Remember the poor, the weak, the helpless, the hungry, the sick, the ill and the bereaved.
Little finger - Pray for yourself. God cares about what you care about and what concerns you.

Slowly trace the pattern of the labyrinth with your finger on the palm of your hand allowing your mind to clear from extra thoughts and focus solely on following the path of the labyrinth.

"Walk" to the centre of the labyrinth and rest momentarily, sharing what is on your mind with God. Take some deep breaths and observe how you are feeling. Retrace your path out of the labyrinth knowing that God is with you and has heard your prayers.

The Lord is near to all who call on him
PSALM 145:18

SAY THE LORD'S PRAYER

Our Father in heaven, hallowed be your name, your kingdom come, your will be done, on earth as in heaven. Give us today our daily bread. Forgive us our sins as we forgive those who sin against us. Lead us not into temptation but deliver us from evil. For the kingdom, the power, and the glory are yours now and for ever. Amen.

> *An example of a prayer station*

Encouraging people to participate and connect

People may walk into your church who have never prayed before. They may find the concept of prayer extremely daunting and not know where to begin. Ensure that you have a simple prayer on display. Introduce a prayer station where visitors are invited to participate in an activity to help them say a prayer, such as a pebble bowl, a stone to hold, to write a prayer or light a candle.

Outside visitors could spot butterflies, count wildflowers, take tree rubbings, discover a labyrinth or sit underneath a tree. These are simple ideas to make visitors feel they are in a welcoming place and encourage them to actively engage with God and with your church. There are no set rules for prayer stations, so be creative. Consider outdoor spaces as well as indoor ones.

Additionally, ensure you have an area where visitors can leave requests for prayer and have a way of showing this is done. This shows visitors that they matter to you and that you care about them.

Ensure that you have a simple prayer on display.

Your church today and a reason to return

Some visitors may think that your church is a beautiful historic building which now stands empty. Think about how you can communicate the life that still exists in your church, and how you can invite them to be part of your church's future.

Do you hold a candlelit carol service at Christmas?

Or a Teddy Bears Parachute Jump off the tower in July?

Or host a regular toddler group?

If you do then shout about it!

Display great photos on an internal noticeboard and on the website, (with the appropriate permissions). If your church is on Facebook, use it for this purpose and promote the page on your church communications. Don't assume that people will read about it in the local magazine.

By the time they leave, every visitor to your church should know when your next service or event is, and how welcome they are.

If your church is on Facebook, use it for this purpose and promote the page on your church communications.

CASE STUDY

Steve Fenning is the Lead Pastor of Forge Church in Suffolk. Steve is the son of a farmer and has always had a passion for rural ministry. The church he leads meets in Debenham and has grown from 24 to 300+ people over the past 30 years (**forgechurch.com**).

Steve on the key to church growth:
"I am often asked why the church has grown, and I think it comes down to several reasons:

1   We are intentional about reaching out to unchurched people and being inclusive in our language. We have a clear vision and a clear mission. People might not like everything we do, but we have a clear purpose and we stick to it.

2   We have put real energy into what we offer to children and young people, employing staff to oversee the kids and youth congregations and being involved in local schools.

3   The physical environment is so important. We invest a huge amount of time and resources into making our kids, youth and adult venues warm, inviting, creative and enjoyable spaces to spend time in. This involves a lot of setting up each week!

4   Maintaining a consistent approach in our worship and teaching style has given the congregation confidence to invite family and friends to services on any week - whether in person or online."

THINKING ABOUT THE SERVICE

Whether your services are online, in person, or both, here are some key points to remember:

> This might be someone's first ever Sunday in your church, so make sure you are designing your services for the lost and not the found. Always assume you have new people coming and make sure they have everything they need.

> Whoever you have up front is who you will attract to your church. So if you want to attract more people in their 20s, try and get someone in their 20s to do the opening welcome. If you want to attract a broad range of people, have several different people welcoming and hosting each week.

> Never assume that people will know who you are, or who other people are. Remember to always introduce yourself and avoid saying things like "Speak to Jane after the service...". Who's Jane?!

> Briefly explain where the toilets are, or if you're online, how to use the chat facility. Explain how long the service will be.

> Never underestimate the power of sparkling toilets! Think flowers and hand lotion, as well as nice handwash.

> Avoid using insider lingo and abbreviations. Don't just assume people know what the PCC is or what 'intercessions' means.

> Explain the meaning of songs before you sing them.

> Explain who the author of the book of the Bible reading is and give some context as to when it was written.

> Keep your sermons authentic and personal, to be enjoyed not endured. People want to see the real you and hear about real struggles and triumphs. That's what Jesus did – he told stories about everyday life.

> Give people a hook for next week's service or a clear next step, such as details of a fun kids' event coming up, a new course starting which will help people explore the Christian faith, or details of how to get in touch.

> The welcome isn't just for the beginning of the service. Ensure people are given a warm 'goodbye' and 'hope to see you again sometime' as they leave.

Angling your welcome

Think carefully and objectively about who your welcome is aimed at. Are you serving the wants and wishes of your current congregation, or are you angling your welcome towards those people who haven't yet stepped inside your church? It is very easy to fall into the habit of serving your current congregation over the needs of newcomers.

Here are two true stories of when a church, without realising it, focused their welcome on their current congregation:

1   It was suggested to a rural churchwarden that it might be more welcoming to have a basket of children's toys and books in the church, to which she replied, "That won't be necessary as we don't have any children in the congregation."

2   During the COVID-19 pandemic, the Diocese of Exeter produced a poster explaining the restrictions and providing contact details if people needed someone to talk to. A churchwarden asked if the contact details section could be removed saying: "There are only about 28 people in the congregation and we all have each other's numbers, so it's not necessary to put any contact details up on a poster."

Both of these people are dedicated and hard-working members of the church, who genuinely want their church to flourish. Their mistake was to focus on the needs of the people who already attended, rather than considering the needs of the many people who didn't.

We need courage to say to the 99 that we are going to make some changes to find the one lost sheep. This may involve going against their preference for the sake of that purpose.

GREAT RESOURCES

Canva is a brilliant online design system which makes it really easy to design attractive posters, flyers, Facebook posts etc: **canva.com**

ReSource: Resources to enable little, local and ordinary churches: **resource-arm.net**

Arthur Rank Centre: arthurrankcentre.org.uk

Rural Ministries: ruralministries.org.uk

The Further Faster Network: furtherfaster.network

New Wine Rural Team: new-wine.org/networks-ministries/rural

Lifewords do some great free Christian resources: lifewords.global/shop

Christian Publishing and Outreach for posters and resources: **cpo.org.uk**

The **Everybody Welcome** course by Bob Jackson and George Fisher from Church House Publishing: chpublishing.co.uk

A free digital welcome supplement - **Everybody Welcome Online** - is available from CPAS: **cpas.org.uk**

Welcome Guide produced by Growing the Rural Church in the Diocese of Exeter: exeter.anglican.org/welcome-resources

LightWave in the Diocese of St Edmundsbury and Ipswich offers all kinds of helpful resources for rural outreach: lightwave.community/resources

God for All is an ecumenical coalition based in Cumbria with lots of outreach resources any church can try: godforall.org.uk/resource-downloads

2

MAKING THE MOST OF LIFE EVENTS

THREE KEY THINGS YOU'LL LEARN IN THIS CHAPTER

> The link between life events and faith journeys, and how you can amplify this.

> Ways to involve lots of people from the church in this ministry and mission.

> The vital importance of keeping in touch with new contacts.

INTRODUCTION

H ere, the Revd Sandra Millar, Head of Life Events for the Church of England from 2013 to 2022 recalls an experience while taking a service in a rural parish that is part of a multi-parish team with 11 churches.

"That Sunday was a shared service and there were just over 60 people present. As I waited for the service to begin, I scanned through the register looking at some of the other numbers. Most Sundays there were around 14 people attending. But suddenly my eye was drawn to some large figures: 87, 93, 76, and at least two that were over 100, including one that was closer to 200. I began to do some sums; it seemed that in the month of June, the church had seen around 500 people attending services – two weddings, two christenings and a funeral. In addition, I knew that the ministry team had been involved in funerals at a local crematorium in that time frame, and that the numbers at those services were simply unrecorded.

But at a conservative guesstimate, it seemed likely that over a month, this little church with a regular Sunday attendance of less than 20, had touched the lives of 650 people, all of whom had had an opportunity to hear the story of God's love and faithfulness."

...the Church of England nationally still meets around 400,000 people every week...

This is not an uncommon story of rural ministry around life events. For generation after generation, churches in villages and hamlets have walked alongside people at the most important and significant moments in their lives, events marked in the timeless rituals of a baptism, a marriage ceremony and a funeral. Although the changing cultural context has seen a decline in numbers seeking out the church at these moments, the Church of England nationally still meets around 400,000 people every week at these events.

Over half the population have been to church for one of these services, and it makes the families at the heart of each event feel connected to church. These are moments with big emotions and big questions, and for many of our small communities, the significance of this ministry is very great.

This chapter will give some practical ideas as to how rural churches can best support families and congregations at these key times, with ideas for resources and stories of things that have worked.

IN THE COMMUNITY – SHOUT FROM THE ROOFTOPS

The knowledge that the church is there for *everyone* is slowly slipping away, and one of the really positive and simple things any church can do is proactively publicise their life events services widely.

There are lots of good communication ideas in Chapter 10 and ways to make your communications feel welcoming in Chapter 1, but telling people that we are there for them in *their* lives, rather than just inviting them to join ours, means including good stories and information in newsletters, websites and social media. Here are two suggestions:

1   **Noticeboards – whether external or internal**. What messages are offered in the village hall and other community venues about the church's welcome and care at life's big moments? Make sure there is clear, attractive material encouraging people to 'just ask' about what the church offers, and find out about how we are there for them. You can find good publicity posters at churchprinthub.org, (enter 'Just Ask' into the search bar to see that collection of resources), along with lots of other leaflets and resources that can be given to new enquirers.

2   **Right church, right event** – think carefully across your church team as to which churches are best suited to which life event. Although every church can offer all, identify those communities where there are young families, or where there is a wedding venue nearby, and develop those places, supporting them with publicity.

PARTNERSHIPS –
TOGETHER IS BETTER

Partnerships – work across your multi-parish church team to build partnerships that generate enquiries from families and couples. These are just a small selection of some easy-win connections you could try:

1   Build good relationships with local funeral directors. It can't be overstated how important it is to be available – if a funeral director doesn't reach someone from the church quickly, they'll offer that funeral to another celebrant, and your opportunity to connect with that family is forever lost, so make sure there is an on-call number that is always answered by one of you.

2   Think about how you might work with a village hall or community space to offer a 'package' for weddings or christenings.

3   If you have a school in your patch, make sure there is good information there, maybe on noticeboards, about how the church supports people for every stage in life.

4   Christianity is part of the school curriculum – could you offer to do a mock wedding or christening, exploring the meanings of the symbols, making good memories, and reminding everyone that church is there for them?

FIRST CONTACT – WARM WORDS BEFORE FORM FILLING

The first time you hear from a family or couple might be directly through an email or a phone call, or indirectly, through a funeral director. The first response is really important. Balance 'process' with 'warmth', which can transform the couple's response and experience, as this diagram shows:

Making relationship:

If someone calls to book a wedding or christening, the first thing to say to them is, "Congratulations!" Find out the story of a family, and then move on to support that relationship with a good process. In rural communities, there may be enquiries from those who are not resident, but still feel connected. That connection could be a bit of family history, or a personal link, such as childhood holidays. For weddings, it may just be that it is near the reception venue. Many non-church people will approach a church just as they would a secular venue, and may ask at more than one church. Warmth means we connect to their story, and then back that up with good information to help them make their decision.

Flourishing funeral ministry

There is a benefice in Gloucestershire which has three parishes plus one additional open churchyard.
When the vicar arrived, she discovered a Reader working as a part-time administrator alongside a full-time job.

As he approached retirement, she asked him if he would like to take a funeral – and he did. Now this Reader has become the church's designated Funeral Minister, and is listed in the magazine and on the website as the Funeral Administrator too.

He is the first point of contact for Funeral Directors and for families, taking most funerals across the benefice, and offering support to other parishes as well. He can be contacted by mobile phone for funerals and other enquiries, and critically, he is always available, giving quality time to preparing, travelling as needed and being there for people.

As the vicar said, *"He knows a lot of people, and is trusted and liked in the community. He didn't realise at first that this was his vocation, but it clearly is, and he is flourishing. We also use the Church of England's Life Events Diary to maintain information and keep in contact with people. Our next step is to make our follow-up more focused and planned with our team of lay pastoral visitors."*

PREPARATION AND PLANNING

Each of the big three life events requires different kinds of planning and each has a different time scale. But whichever it is, those involved will go away with treasured memories if it feels personal, rather than a 'one-size-fits-all' solution.

› **Create a team to help families** with planning and preparing, whether organising a rehearsal for the day itself, or offering time to reflect on the meaning of marriage vows or baptism promises.

› **Develop a culture of prayer** around life events: this could mean making sure that every event (and its anniversary) is included in a pewsheet or newsletter, but could also mean people praying on the day, or for a family in the weeks leading up to their day. Anyone in the church can do this! Something as simple as a card which includes a prayer can be really important to a family or a couple, reminding them that you are praying and that they can pray too. You could also create a prayer area in church or churchyard focused around the event. For these and many other ideas on involving everyone in prayer, see churchsupporthub.org.

> **Becoming a church that blesses**: one of the best ways of making connections between church and families is through simple gifts. Even the smallest congregation

or community can offer creative skills for this. For example, knitting squares to make shawls for children being baptised, or creating a little 'treasure box' with names on to give to a wedding couple. And there are all kinds of ways in which cake-making builds relationship – whether dropped round to someone grieving, or taken as thanks to the funeral director staff, or the playgroup leaders – it all helps to make those connections which build a sense that the church is there for people.

> TIP: Don't forget that even a banns reading can be special. Many couples and their families treasure the moment when banns are read, so make sure you invite the couple and their parents or grandparents to come and listen.

ON THE BIG DAY

Many life event services can feel quite disconnected from the local worshipping congregation and the community, even christenings (if they are outside the main Sunday service). Funerals at crematoria are also remote from the parish, although the person who has died may have many links to the local church and village life.

> **Presence** – think about how the church can connect to the event. One or two people who are there being welcoming and friendly helps to show the church as more than a building. There are other occasions, apart from the christening, wedding or funeral itself, where families may come to church again. For example, at a regular service for remembering those who have died, make sure there are one or two people looking out for those who are unfamiliar.

> **People** – Weddings, funerals and christenings are a huge opportunity for people to experience church, many of them for the first time, and many of them in age groups that are not regularly seen in a local church. Make sure that the church is ready to welcome the guests of those who are at the heart of the service. Good practical information on the day (especially if you don't have toilets!) helps. Take time to loiter and speak to people as they arrive. Each event will also have people who are especially important – at a funeral, there may be friends, family, long-standing neighbours; at weddings, there are close family, and at christenings there are godparents, and honouring and recognising them is particularly important.

Take time to loiter and speak to people as they arrive.

> **Your story, their story, God's story** – remember that the family or couple have specifically chosen to be in church, *your* church for their event, so reflect the links between the story of that place and the story of those who are coming, and weave that into the way God loves and watches over all our relationships, our connections and our comings and goings.

INTO THE FUTURE –
IT'S NEVER ALL OVER

DID YOU KNOW? Church of England research discovered that nine out of 10 of those who have shared one of their life events with a church would like to hear from us again. Maintaining contact is more likely to result in the contact returning to church and potentially growing in their faith.

What does 'hearing from us again' mean in a rural setting, both for those who live there and for those who are passing through?

> **Little church, big church** – life events services make a key connection between a relationship that someone has with *your* church and the relationship they have with the *whole* Church of England. You may be aware that there are those who pop into your church when out for a walk, or on holiday, or visiting friends, to have a look round, and then light a candle or write a prayer. We are there for people wherever they go, whatever their need, for as long as they need us. So, remind those you meet of that link with a card on anniversaries, a message, an email, a newsletter, a poster in church, spaces for people to remember loved ones inside and outside the church. Even if those contacts live many miles away, we are still here for them, and it will remind them that their local church is also. For many families and couples, we will probably never know where that leads, but we have discovered that if we keep in touch, they may return. But if we don't, then not only will they not come back, they will also be disappointed that they didn't hear from us again.

> **Free admin help** – one of the best ways of keeping track of those you meet at weddings, funerals, christenings and banns services is by using the free Church of England online admin tool, lifeeventsdiary. org. It is adaptable to the local parish arrangement, including multi-parish benefices, teams and all the permutations of organisation we have. Check it out – there is ample online training and support too.

> **Inform, invite, involve** – keeping in touch is not just about routinely putting the parish magazine through a letterbox, or dropping off the leaflet with all the complicated array of Christmas services on offer. Sit on your hands and resist giving too many choices – just invite certain people to one thing. For example, those who are bereaved may be available to attend a mid-week service. One of your villages might have a toddler group – let families with young children know. Back up the information with specific invites, for example, send all your baptism families a focused invitation to a crib service or the harvest festival. Tailored printed invitations for all sorts of things are on churchprinthub.org.

Involving people means accepting their offers of help, or asking them to help. Helping makes people move from outsider to insider. In research with couples attending church to qualify to marry, things like being asked to carry up the communion elements or the offering were found to be very significant.

> **Using festivals for follow up** – there are many special moments in the church calendar – Palm Sunday, Pentecost, Advent Sunday and more. Some of these are great for inviting families to come along, as well as special moments in the secular or cultural calendar (see Chapter 7). Could Valentine's Day be a chance to invite those married at your church, or getting ready to marry, to come to a fun social? It might also be a chance to open a church with reflective space, even a remembering service, for those who have been bereaved of a life partner.

> **Their life story** – dates that are personally relevant especially in the journey of grief, might include anniversaries or birthdays. For families with children, it might be starting school, for couples it could be 'one year till your wedding day'. The Life Events Diary lets you keep track of all these dates, so you can send a card or an invitation, either to a service, to visit church, or even to meet someone for coffee.

> **Never give up** – one of the hardest things for any church is the sense that we are sending communications and nothing is happening. Very often we lose confidence and assume that people don't want to hear from us anymore. But church has been part of their life story, and although it might take years, and it might not be your church, it is up to them to 'unsubscribe'. So keep going – and every time an email, or a card, or an invite is sent, the person sending it can offer a prayer for that family. Think of all those years when people prayed for names on a Cradle Roll – many of us are where we are today because of those prayers.

CASE STUDY

Wedding partners make an impact

Reader Carolyn Wort at the very pretty St Mary's Church, Whitewell, in Cheshire, has promoted church weddings in partnership with a local civil wedding venue for several years, having a stand at their regular wedding fairs. She said initially the PCC and others weren't sure if it was the right thing to be doing, but as the church built up its wedding ministry, it was taking around 20-30 weddings each year pre-pandemic. Around 80% of those were for couples who lived outside the parish, either making a connection by attending or by another Marriage Measure connection.

Carolyn takes the view that the mission opportunities are great, and she sees many couples return for baptism as their families grow, or return to ask for the church's involvement in family funerals.

The younger demographic of couples attending also meant the church adjusted their worship style to take that into account and that this had driven amazing and beneficial change. Everything from sermons to music were modernised and an internet connection was secured so that YouTube videos could be played. This really enhanced the worship and Christian reflection in ways that younger people could relate to.

And Carolyn has no misgivings about couples who don't return to St Mary's – she says it's 'kind of exciting' not to know what happens next in their faith journeys, since she knows they've heard the Gospel through St Mary's and that God can work with that wherever they are.

Aside from the huge missional opportunities, the increase in weddings boosted St Mary's financial income to the point where they could pay the parish share with some still left over.

They used some of this to employ a church cleaner, but the church drew on most of the surplus to tide them over the pandemic when weddings couldn't happen.

The growing reputation for weddings at the church has also boosted interest from more local couples. Carolyn's next focus is building relationships with banns couples and welcoming them to a broad range services and events over and above those where their banns are read.

CONCLUSION

Being there for people at their big life moments has been the bedrock of much rural ministry, and many are the people whose first contact with church begins this way. This ministry affects those who come and those who offer it. "I am in a really rural context" said a vicar, talking about christenings, "and we only baptised three children last year." Then the penny dropped for her, and she looked up and added, "and all three families are now involved in the life of the church!" That is a 100% return, which is staggering, but easily overlooked in a village. New contacts bring new life to those who discover something of the good news of God's love for themselves, but also new life to congregations, where one couple, one family, one new person is an identifiable joy.

"New contacts bring new life to those who discover something of the good news of God's love for themselves, but also new life to congregations, where one couple, one family, one new person is an identifiable joy."

GREAT RESOURCES

churchsupporthub.org – offers insights, ideas, articles, downloads and links.

churchprinthub.org – offers a huge range of specially-produced printed resources to support your life events ministry. If you're thinking of reviewing your ministry, this booklet is a great starting point: churchprinthub.org/pccbooklet.

lifeeventsdiary.org – helps you to streamline all the necessary admin for your life events services and to support you in keeping in contact with the new people you're meeting.

lossandhope.org – to help your church reach out to bereaved people and become more 'bereavement-friendly', including details of how to offer bereavement support through The Bereavement Journey, (see thebereavementjourney.org).

Sites you can refer your contacts to:

For those wanting comprehensive information about church weddings and blessings – yourchurchwedding.org

For those seeking information about christenings and thanksgivings – churchofengland.org/christenings

For those needing information about arranging a church-led funeral – churchofengland.org/funerals

For people who are grieving – ataloss.org

3

USING BUILDINGS CREATIVELY

THREE KEY THINGS YOU'LL LEARN IN THIS CHAPTER

> Your ancient church buildings are a huge asset, just the way they are.

> Your buildings provide limitless, creative opportunities to connect with your village community, and welcome them into the church space, and even into the life of the church.

> There are ways to share the responsibility and cost of caring for your buildings more widely across the community.

INTRODUCTION

Your churches are probably the oldest buildings in their villages, and as such, time has taken its toll on them. They're probably cold in winter and smell a bit fusty. They've probably had many a roof leak. Their walls may well be lined with cracks and peeling paint.

What's more, it's likely they are cared for by just a few people in your local community who are regularly fundraising. If you don't have one of the few churches with an adequate toilet, you may well have that as number one on the wish list.

Your village churches and their list of ailments are among thousands of village churches across England in exactly the same boat. It is easy to be worn down by the maintenance, or even just the thought of it, and to perceive these ancient structures as nothing other than a liability and a burden.

But, despite the great challenges of church upkeep, your congregations are still very attached to them. The same is true of many people in the village community who don't ever, or hardly ever, attend services. Most church leaders have heard a story of a church closure that was met with consternation and strong opposition, with the local press reporting on how a village community is 'up in arms' about the fact that their beloved church is going to be shut and potentially redeveloped into flats, or a pub. It's just the sort of story that seems to happen in our English villages.

But why do churches stir up such emotion? Why would people who seldom go there feel such a deep sense of loss when it disappears?

There may be a variety of reasons, but at the heart of it we sense that it's because church buildings are special to people in a way that no other type of building is.

Village churches have a connection with village life throughout its history. They were built for local people, often by local people. They are places that point towards God and provide space for people to meet Him – through the architecture, through worship, through the peace and tranquillity they offer, through the people who pass in and out of the doors.

Big life events, each with big emotions and big questions around them, happen inside churches. Strong memories are therefore made there. The same applies to significant festivals – Christmas, Easter and Remembrance Day. These are moments in the year when people are drawn to their church, sometimes for reasons of tradition, but sometimes also to draw near with faith, however vague or undefined that faith may be. That is why these are some of the most well-attended services across the year.

So churches have touched the lives of families throughout the generations. They hold meaning and memories. The building, along with its churchyard, its fixtures and fittings, its art, its windows and its weathered old walls, all speak of that connection and local story.

It is why churches are for everyone, and not just for those who faithfully attend week after week. If you ask the people who live in your village what they value about your village churches, in their own way, they will tell you these things.

And yet, if you are one of the few people in your village managing the practicalities of your church buildings, it can feel very hard going at times.

This chapter is about thinking creatively about how you might view your village churches as assets, that might draw people into the worshipping life of your church, often through finding ways to use it differently and encouraging a wider sharing of responsibility for their care.

FOCUS ON WHAT'S POSSIBLE NOW

How many times have you heard (or said yourself), "If only we had a kitchen and a toilet, we could…"?

Whilst it's fair to say that modern facilities can make a difference to the overall comfort of the church, having a toilet and/or kitchen will not in themselves bring people in.

People come through the church doors primarily because of relationships, not facilities. Those relationships will have many different faces – a member of the congregation; a family member

Photo credit: © Kate Sharp / CCT

or friend; a need to seek or rediscover the One who has seemed out of reach; even the building itself exerts a pull on people – that is one reason why churches have value for tourism.

We would all love a reordering project, but they require huge amounts of energy and money. For the congregations of many village churches, the idea of project managing, fundraising and coping with the disruption (and sometimes opposition) of reordering, it can simply feel 'too much' to deal with. If that's you, join the club! This is not a sign of failure or apathy, but a reflection of the enormity of reordering. The good news is that regardless of whether reordering is possible now, or soon, or in a few years, or never, there are things you can do now with the building, just as it is, that will enable you to extend a wider, warmer welcome and connect with new people.

Without major building work, your village church can (and might already!) be used creatively for many things such as:

> traditional and contemporary worship
> reflective and interactive prayer
> foodbank drop off/collections
> befriending services
> community book-swaps
> concerts
> talks and exhibitions...

The key thing is for your congregation to decide how you want to 'be' the church in your village and focus your energies on the activities that are going to support that.

So, what does that look like in practice?

WONDERFUL WORSHIP

Your village church was built first and foremost as a space to worship God. With the constant issues of maintenance and fundraising, it can be hard to keep sight of this. The question here is:
How can we offer worship that's open and accessible for as many people as possible in our village?

The answer doesn't lie in trying to offer everything for everyone in 60 minutes on a Sunday morning. It may be that you need to review your worship and make some adjustments, and/or perhaps even offer an additional service that meets different needs. These are some things to think about:

> How would your worship feel to someone who is deaf or hard of hearing, partially sighted or blind?

> How would your worship come across to someone who is generally unfamiliar with church? Would they know where to sit, what they need in order to follow the service? Would they know any of the hymns/songs or know how to find a Bible passage?

> What do you think children of different ages would think of your worship? Have you asked any of them?

> How comfortable is the worship service for those who are in wheelchairs, or for people who are in some kind of pain when sitting, standing or moving?

When thinking about different needs, it is often very useful to talk to people who have those needs and ask them what would make a difference, (see Chapter 5 on *Being the Heartbeat of a Village Community* for ideas on consulting your community).

Think about which services work in your church building and which don't. You may have several churches in your joint team and therefore have a choice of buildings, each of which is suited to different types of service.

Those that bring lots of people in might well be ones that mark the seasons of the year and life events, and for which your largest church building provides a wonderful atmosphere.

On a freezing grey day in February, it might actually be more welcoming to decamp together to the warmest church, or even to the more modern surroundings of your village hall, if you have one. So much the better if hot drinks can be on standby too!

During hot weather, people may be glad of a cool church to sit in.

It may be that you don't have a service in every village every week. It's ok to offer a variety of venues. Just make sure what you are doing is well-publicised both via traditional posters and however your village communicates upcoming events online. See Chapter 10 for more about communicating well.

And if you were forced to move services online during the COVID-19 pandemic, virtual worship may have an ongoing part to play too, even if just occasionally. Who might tune in to those, and for what reason? Think about how this might influence the kind of worship you offer.

OPEN WIDE

Your village churches have been community spaces for as long as they have been standing. Somehow though, despite those occasions when they are full, it can seem like their spaces are primarily cared for and used by the regular churchgoers. Your churches are already supporting community life through services and life events (see Chapter 2), but there are lots of ways that can be broadened without huge costs. The questions here are:

What needs do our villages have?

How might our church buildings be used to help meet these?

You may already have a pretty good idea of the needs, but asking these questions in your community presents a perfect opportunity to build relationships and to break down any sense that the church building is for (and the responsibility of) a few.

NB You might be worried that in asking people what their needs are, it will be incumbent on you to have to meet them all! Not at all. It's about framing the conversation with your community to ask what you, together, can collectively do with the space your church building provides, to benefit as many people as possible.

> TIP: For ideas on how to have a conversation with your community (often called a 'community consultation') see Chapter 5 on *Being the Heartbeat of a Village Community*. You can also try the Diocese of Hereford's 'Crossing the Threshold Toolkit' – search on hereford.anglican.org.

Don't be afraid to ask

If your village is like most others, there will be a core of community-minded people at the forefront of the parish council, PCC, social club, sports pavilion, village hall or whatever other community assets your villages enjoy.

Many people will wear several hats and it is likely that more helping hands would be hugely welcomed. Having a public conversation about the needs of your village and the church's role in a collective response to those needs not only builds relationships, but it also provides the opportunity for you to ask people to share their skills and get involved.

> TIP: It's a good idea to be as specific as you can about help that is needed. Take time to understand where the skill/time gaps are within your own congregation, so when ideas emerge you can be clear what help will be needed to realise them. And don't be afraid to form joint church/village steering or working groups to take forward ideas. These ensure shared responsibility and accountability.

Get real

You may be thinking this all sounds lovely, aspirational and rather idealised. Your churches' reality, however, is that you have a significant insurance premium, costly heating and need to raise £10,000 to fix the roof, before you can even contemplate meeting any other needs your village may have. It's ok to make this part of the conversation with your community too.

Work with your PCC Treasurer to have ready an easily understood account of your churches' finances and weave the reality of this into your conversation with your community. It is very possible to generate ways forward that combine meeting the existing skills gaps and financial needs of your churches with the broader needs identified by your community.

> DID YOU KNOW? Most people don't know how devolved the funding of parish churches is across England, nor the likely reality that a small number of people shoulder a significant financial burden to keep their village church open to all. They assume the Church of England is wealthy, or receives automatic Government funding, so use community consultation to clarify the reality.

What about faith?

Be mindful of the opportunities to draw more people into discovering or re-discovering the Christian faith. Alongside planning and how you are going to have a conversation with your community about primarily social needs, consider too how you will respond when people demonstrate an interest in spiritual matters. Your congregation may want to think about a short course or reading material on how to support faith enquirers. Many churches have access to mission advisers in their regional networks (at the Diocesan offices of the Church of England for example) who can advise on this.

CASE STUDY

St Mary the Virgin, Stannington, Northumberland

St Mary the Virgin church serves a small parish with a population of around 1,500 people. The PCC had a vision to make the church a centre for broader family life through educational and social activities, but the building needed significant repairs.

Castle Morpeth Borough Council was also looking for a centre to provide free access to computers and IT tuition for local residents, so this became a natural partnership to start from.

The church raised £350,000, which included private donations, funders such as English Heritage, fundraising events and significant loans. Within five years, the money was raised and the essential work was completed. Loans have now been repaid.

An IT learning suite was located at the foot of the bell tower. This included computers for local people to access and to have computer literacy tuition. It ran well for several years until it came to a natural end, but the room continues to be used as a church office and print room.

The rest of the improvements in the church made social functions more possible, transforming mission and ministry. Events and functions remain one of the church's key methods of outreach and it has a very active social committee. Church warden Brian Smiles says that without these events at the church, there would be little else happening in the village that brings people together in quite the same way.

More recently, a Post Office has been operating in the church and it also has a coffee shop.

A STITCH IN TIME...

Engaging in a conversation about creative use of your village churches is interesting, exciting and future-focused. Just as future-focused, but perhaps less glamorous, is the ongoing work of managing the building itself. Though the day-to-day reality of being custodians of an ancient building can be daunting, it is a precious task entrusted to you by past generations, not only for the present community, but for the communities of your villages in the future.

If you have ever spent time with a conservation professional, they will tell you that regular maintenance of heritage buildings is vital. It's really all about keeping water out, and small repairs now can prevent larger problems in the future, saving money in the long run. This is not a new idea. An inscription dated 1634 in a Norfolk church tower reads:

This church was built in it God to adore, and ought to have been repaired long before, by which neglect we did great sums expend. Then let successors look in time to mend, for if decays they early don't prevent, they will like us when 'tis too late, repent.

Photo credit: © George Reynolds / CCT

... regular maintenance of heritage buildings is vital.

Putting in place a regular maintenance programme which attends to basic things like roof tiles and gutters really does make a difference. Your village church is most likely part of a multi-parish grouping (benefice) and you will all be facing the same maintenance issues. Might your benefice or deanery work together to engage a regular contractor? This will lighten the administration load and reduce costs.

> TIP: Overseeing maintenance is also a task that an interested member of your community might be willing to get involved in. You won't know unless you ask for help, so include this in a conversation with your community.

CASE STUDY

St Giles, Langford, Essex

St Giles is a Grade II listed building and the church serves a tiny parish of around 170 people. One of the churchwardens, Irene Allen, entered a competition in the local magazine 'Essex matters', which asked the question, 'What would you do for your community if you had £10,000?'. Her entry suggested extending the use of the church building to incorporate a small village shop, and the entry was one of the winners.

With the £10,000 prize money, the shop, later named 'Heavenly Supplies', was created in the church's vestry. There were virtually no building works as such, but some changes were made to incorporate shelving, improve lighting and provide signage.

The project was tackled in partnership with Essex County Council, the Diocesan Advisory Committee, the Rural Community Council of Essex and the Parish Council. It took 18 months to complete from beginning to end. A lot of this time was in waiting for the legal approval to proceed.

The current vicar, the Revd Asa Humphreys, said the shop had been a lifeline for villagers during the pandemic, enabling the church to be at the forefront of supporting those in need. The shop offers a range of essential items you'd expect to find in a village convenience store, and the church was able to organise grocery deliveries on request for those isolating and/or those unable to shop online.

But, Asa explained, the shop has innumerable, long-term benefits for both the community and the church, including:

> Enabling people to see inside the church who would not have otherwise, since the building always had to be locked to meet insurance obligations. Now, people can see inside and this has nurtured a community affection for the building and a desire to protect it. Not only that, it has helped people to feel welcome and comfortable in the building, which in turn develops confidence so that newcomers might come along to publicised services.

> After services, people tend to linger for longer as they top up on store cupboard items at the shop. It offers a reason to remain in the church, which lengthens conversations, and therefore helps relationships to develop. Asa felt this had helped to broaden the 'fringe' contacts of the church as well as deepen relationships with existing contacts. For a fairly small and spread-out village, he felt this was essential to help combat loneliness too.

> The shop is used by walkers, which again makes the building accessible and welcoming to a wider set of contacts.

Asa said, "It initially felt strange to robe up in the vestry surrounded by Mars Bars and tinned tomatoes, but our little shop is a testament to God's good planning and a reminder of how vital the church is in this context. It's practical love in action; we're incredibly proud of it, and so grateful for Irene's steadfast dedication and God's amazing provision."

CONCLUSION

From the flickering candles of the carol service, to the buzzing bees in the summer churchyard, to the local produce given at harvest, your church buildings are year-round, much-loved assets to your villages. With a little creative thought and planning, they provide brilliant opportunities to connect with your village community, through which you may draw people both into the worshipping life of your church, and find ways to share the responsibility of caring for your building for now and the future.

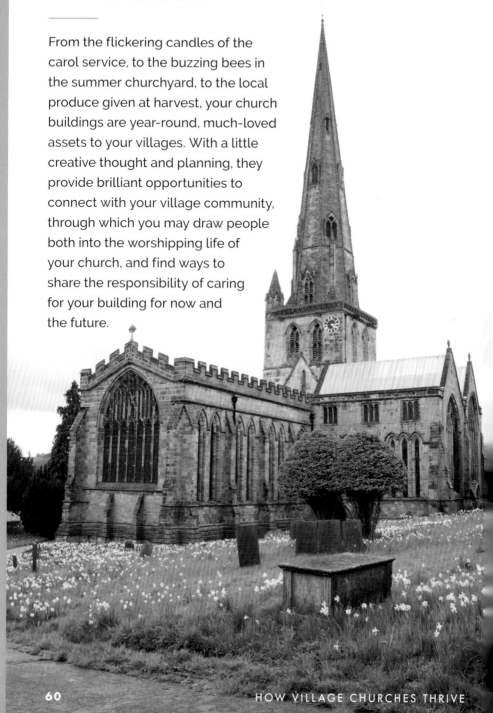

GREAT RESOURCES

ChurchCare on the national Church of England website has some excellent pages to explore, see churchofengland.org/churchcare. These include:

> A 'Building maintenance and repair' section which offers a 'Calendar of care' to download and keep your maintenance on track.

> A whole section on funding and grants for church buildings.

> Help and advice on how to take action on the environment and reduce your church's carbon footprint.

> Case studies of church buildings creatively used.

The Diocese of Hereford's 'Crossing the Threshold Toolkit' offers a step-by-step guide to manage a church building project. Search 'Threshold' on hereford.anglican.org.

maintenancebooker.org.uk is a website developed to make it easier for churchwardens and other volunteers to find recommended and qualified contractors to improve the maintenance of their buildings.

4

CARING FOR GOD'S ACRE

—

THREE KEY THINGS YOU'LL LEARN IN THIS CHAPTER

> Why churchyards draw people and how you can build on their interest.

> How you can engage the whole community in the love and care of your churchyard.

> Churchyards can be a visible expression of one of the Church of England's five marks of mission: 'To strive to safeguard the integrity of creation, and sustain and renew the life of the earth.'

INTRODUCTION

T

he 2020s have really focused our minds on large and seemingly intractable problems; global warming, extinction of rare species and more recently, a pandemic. During this time, restrictions and limitations on leaving our local areas have also focused people's attention on their immediate community and the green spaces within it, recognised as essential for wellbeing.

As a result, we have seen people developing a new interest in their locality and in particular, a longing to improve places for exploring in the fresh air and providing habitats for wildlife.

Not only that, we have also seen evidence of people becoming more community-minded, with online social media groups coming into their own, neighbours supporting each other with errands, odd jobs and giveaways, and an enthusiasm for sharing and caring that we have not really seen in recent decades.

Having had to face the fragility of jobs, relationships, and health, you may have noticed too that people are tending to appreciate what really matters in life. If people haven't had to face crises in these areas (and many have), then they have had time to reflect, take stock and appreciate simplicity, beauty in nature nearby, and connections with family, friends and neighbours.

In many ways, a rural churchyard encompasses all of these concepts. Our churchyards are, or have the potential to be, rich in green space, biodiversity and a place to think about the big questions in life. This is literally a natural draw for people.

> One of the most enduring texts from the 18th Century is Thomas Gray's *Elegy written in a country churchyard*. It depicts a churchyard as a wild and disordered place; a place where the tensions between human culture and the natural world are intertwined and, while people die, the natural world goes on.

Over half of the visitors to churchyards do not actually cross the threshold of the church building and are not necessarily visiting the grave of a loved one. They are spending time in this special place simply because they enjoy being there.

When asked what makes it special, reasons include:

Peace, Nature, Memories, Birdsong, Wild Flowers, Trees, Butterflies

(The Nature of God's Acre by Miles King and Mark Betson, published by The Nature of God's Acre Project Team 2014, and their copyright. ISBN 978-0-9931545-0-8)

Clearly the natural environment in a churchyard is greatly appreciated, but note that among the references to nature, there is a clear indication that churchyards hold something deeper for people too. Survey respondents articulate this as 'memories' and that word can mean many different things to different people.

Might they be remembering the events
that have taken place in the church and
at which they were present? Or that simply
strolling through the churchyard transports
them back to a significant moment? Or has
someone they love now died and been
buried in the churchyard – is it a precious
space for remembering them?

Or might it be that the old headstones all
around carry stories of the lives of local
people back down the generations?
Local history is there for all to see.

Perhaps it is a combination of all these things. What is clear is that people genuinely love and cherish churchyards and could be willing to be a part of their care.

But on a deeper level, Christians point to nature as evidence of a loving, creator God, limitless in diversity and the source of all life's flourishing. In the Gospels we hear Jesus speak of looking at the 'birds of the air' and 'lilies of the field' to tell us about what is important in our lives and what to strive for (Matthew 6.25-34).

Headstones speak of love, of the heartache of loss, but also of the Christian hope that God is with us in our suffering and that death is not the end.

To see a beautiful example of this, visit churchofengland.org and search 'baby loss memorial' to read the moving story of The Revds Jenny and Jim Bridgman.

With all this in mind, put simply, our churchyards are places where people think about God. This chapter helps you create a space that enables that connection to happen and honours the beauty and holiness of 'God's Acre'.

St. John the Baptist Church, Hope Bagot, Shropshire, in partnership with the Stourport Ramblers.

(Dedicated to the late Charles Kenchington who drove this brilliant initiative, and who is mentioned and quoted here.)

"We were struggling with the amount of grass to cut and rake up; a few of us were trying to get the work done but were in despair with the amount of grass to manage. We were on the lookout for help from any quarter."

Around this time, the Stourbridge Ramblers were on a walk in the area and stopped for lunch. Charles knew one of them, so invited them all to have a drink in his garden. He then asked them if they would come back next year and help with the churchyard for half a day.

The following year the Ramblers arrived with their own gardening tools and raked up the grass which had been cut a week earlier. After they raked it, a local farmer came and baled it. The villagers made a large lunch with several puddings and cider to celebrate and to thank the Ramblers.

This arrangement has lasted for about 20 years. The Ramblers visit the church at other times of the year including the Christmas Carol service. They read Lessons and even bring raffle prizes.

The site now has a wide variety of plants and has been designated a Local Wildlife Site because of its richness for wildlife.

BIODIVERSITY AND THE PASSAGE OF TIME

Your churchyard may be the oldest piece of enclosed land in the parish, and perhaps the wall surrounding it hasn't changed much over the centuries.

We also know that although churchyards have connotations with death, they are actually teeming with life.

> **DID YOU KNOW?** Some churchyards contain quite amazing numbers of species, possibly over 1,000 different ones?

This richness of life has evolved over centuries and is absolutely fascinating to understand. Spending some time really noticing what is already in your churchyard will help you to highlight it to all visitors and engage their interest.

A brief look at the history of rural churchyards in Britain may help you with this.

Ancient churchyards

It is likely that many of our rural churchyards pre-date the current church building; sometimes churches and churchyards actually replaced, or were attached, to pre-existing pagan sites.

Do you have a veteran or ancient yew tree in your churchyard? This can indicate an ancient sacred site as some of these wonderful trees are thought to predate Christianity in Britain and in some cases the birth of Christ.

Whilst it is difficult to accurately assess tree age, experts have grouped them into three overlapping categories:

Notable Yews	300 to 800 years old
Veteran Yews	500 to 1,200 years old
Ancient Yews	At least 800 years old with no known upper age limit

It was Pope Gregory the Great (590AD) who recommended churchyards as burial places, so that worshippers walked past graves and remembered the dead in their prayers. The area of one acre for burial was laid down in 943 by the Welsh king Hywel Dda, so by the C10th 'God's Acre' was being marked by wooden crosses in churchyard corners or enclosed within a sheltering hedge or wall.

Signs of ancient history

1 **Higher ground inside the churchyard**
    Take a look at the level of the ground within your churchyard compared to that beyond the wall.
    Is it higher? There are thought to be the remains of about 10,000 burials in an old churchyard, an idea guaranteed to make your local school children squeal!

2 **Glorious greens**
    When we think of grassland or a lawn, we may imagine a monotonous green colour. The grassland within a churchyard can be quite different, it has the potential to chart a spectrum of changing colours as flowers, seeds, grasses and fungi appear over the seasons. Previous generations would have viewed this kaleidoscope as normal; it is in the last 60 years that we have become accustomed to a greatly reduced colour palette.

3 A lichen laboratory

Monuments marking graves became fashionable in churchyards in the 18th and 19th centuries and remain so. The churchyard becomes an embodiment of the social history of your community from then on.

This was also a fantastic boost for lichens, particularly in areas without natural rocky outcrops, so now a lichenologist on holiday goes straight to the nearest churchyard to see what is growing.

4 A home for the vulnerable

Within the sheltering wall or hedge of the churchyard, many plants and animals which were common a few decades ago but are now at risk, can still be found. Do you have swifts, swallows and house martins swooping about in the summer? When did you last see a hedgehog? Churchyards are brilliant for them. Are there slow worms and toads hunting for slugs at the base of the wall, or lizards basking on the top?

"But we don't have to limit ourselves to social studies or historical investigation when in the company of the dead on a visit to a cemetery...I plan to keep on visiting, first of all for the dog – that is certainly what I tell the children – but really for me, for that reassuring sense my walks give me that I am part of a human chain, going through the cycle of birth and death as those who came before, and will come after me." [1]

This quote from Peter Stanford's book *How to Read a Graveyard* highlights the opportunity an ancient churchyard presents about linking visitors with a timeless God – the God of Abraham, Isaac and Jacob – and the God of our ancestors buried here. Bible passages

---

[1] Peter Stanford, *How to read a Graveyard: Journeys in the company of the dead*, p.241.

reaffirming God's presence with us can be displayed in creative ways in churchyards – from laminated posters to collages of natural materials. The Church Support Hub has posters and ideas – visit churchsupporthub.org and search there for 'outdoor spaces'.

Younger churchyards

It is since WWII that we have lost so much of our biodiversity, in particular our meadows. If your churchyard was consecrated before the 1960s, it is likely to contain this precious meadow habitat. If consecrated later, or if it has suffered poor management practices in the past, don't despair – you have a clean slate on which to create something special...

CARING TOGETHER

For many churches, the churchyard may have become something of a burden. Perhaps you had a larger group of churchyard volunteers in the past and this is now reduced, so the jobs fall to a smaller number of you now. If you pay a contractor, there may be times when you struggle to make ends meet.

By changing the way that you manage your churchyard it is possible to reduce the work needed, bring in new volunteers, perhaps including younger people who are interested in nature conservation, whilst still maintaining a churchyard which looks loved and cared for. Start with these five ideas. The Caring for God's Acre website will help at all stages: caringforgodsacre.org.uk.

CASE STUDY

Bishops Castle Primary School at St John the Baptist Church, Bishops Castle, Shropshire.

Patrick Harris, a teacher of a class of 8/9 year olds at the school said: "We wanted to combine an educational visit to the local churchyard with science learning, and also habitat creation within our school grounds."

Patrick and Harriet Carty from Caring for God's Acre met up to see which activities within the Education Pack would be best suited. The class were covering invertebrates and taxonomy in Biology, including working with keys. They looked at the mini-beast section of the pack and selected: Top Tips for *Mini-beast Hunting; Mini-beast Identification Key; Take a Closer Look* and *Building a Bug Hotel.*

Each child took a clipboard with a copy of the Top Tips. They also took butterfly sweep nets, white trays, pooters and magnifying boxes, along with a tablet for photographing mini-beasts.

After exploration and discussion, the group agreed that when they returned to school, they would create a bug hotel.

The visit helped to bring the subject to life for the children and they enjoyed both aspects of the day; looking at invertebrates and building the bug hotel.

It is worth noting that several of the children wanted to talk about deceased relatives buried in the churchyard and so a listening adult was helpful.

FIVE WAYS TO WELCOME WILDLIFE TO YOUR CHURCHYARD

1 **Create a mini meadow**

Choose an area of grass which is in full sun and which is currently mown short. Leave it uncut for about 14 weeks over the spring and summer. See how many wildflowers come up naturally, you will probably be surprised. These will attract bees and butterflies. When deciding where to have a flowery meadow, a good rule of thumb is to imagine what the churchyard looked like when the people buried there were alive. People from Georgian, Victorian or Edwardian times would have been used to a churchyard that was managed for hay, cut with scythes and grazed with sheep or a pony after the hay cut. The short, manicured grass that we have now is created by repeated mowing, so people from the 1960s onwards would have been familiar with this appearance.

Scythe or strim the long grass, rake it up and remove it to a compost heap or use it to make hay.

Take a look at the Caring for God's Acre Action Pack Sheets A2, A3 & A8, (on the website), to learn how to create and manage a meadow.

2 **Help old trees by looking after their roots**

Veteran and ancient trees are like a Noah's Ark for many wildlife species. Gently clear below these trees, removing young saplings, piles of grass cuttings, sheds, grave spoil, old bottles and anything else that is there. Remove ivy from yew trees, (but often there is no need to do so from other species unless advised to by an arboricultural expert).

There's a Caring for God's Acre Action Pack to help you learn about veteran and ancient trees.

3 **Give wildlife a home by making habitat boxes, deadwood piles and compost bays**
Consider putting swift boxes behind the louvres in the church tower. Erect a range of different sized bird boxes, including open fronted ones for Spotted Flycatcher and Robin. Put bat boxes up in trees, (seek advice on location first).

Hedgehogs, amphibians such as frogs and newts, and reptiles such as slow worm, all love deadwood piles and compost heaps, using them to hunt for snails, beetles, worms and other invertebrates. Create a pile of deadwood in a shady place using logs and twigs of a variety of sizes. Compost your grass cuttings.

Share the news of wildlife progress on social media – especially if there are photos!

Take a look at the Caring for God's Acre Action Pack sheets A8 for more ideas.

4 **Be a little untidy**
Try to have an area of tussocky grassland or scrub, perhaps against a wall or round the back, away from the church entrance. Cut and clear this back every two or three years, doing a section each year. This will be fantastic shelter and great for overwintering invertebrates as well as amphibians and reptiles. Hedgehogs love places like this too.

5 Plant for pollinators

Make sure your flowerbeds or plant
pots contain species that are useful
to insects. Native plants and grasses,
plus both early spring and autumn
flowering species are ideal, providing
nectar and pollen for many months
of the year. How about planting some
herbs such as rosemary, chives and
marjoram which people can enjoy
too? The wildflower Viper's Bugloss
is outstanding for insects and very
attractive too.

FIVE WAYS TO WELCOME PEOPLE TO YOUR CHURCHYARD

Many people who manage churchyards are worried about what other people will think about changes to the appearance of the site, in particular by allowing some areas of grassland to grow long and fill with wildflowers. Whilst surveys show that most people will welcome these changes, some will not, and may fear that the churchyard is becoming neglected. It is possible to strike a balance here, so follow these five steps to show that you are welcoming people as well as wildlife.

1 **Make a plan**
   Draw up a management plan using the Caring for God's Acre system in the Action Pack (Sheet A1 – 5 Steps to Churchyard and Burial Ground Care). This involves the local community and reassures people that the churchyard is being cared for, and that there are reasons for any changes they may notice. It is a simple, map-based plan with a timetable of jobs that all can join in with.

2 **Keep short, mown grass in key areas**
   Mow regularly around the church building, on either side of surfaced paths, where there are current graves and war graves. Mow meandering paths through your meadow areas. Collect the grass cuttings when you mow – this is good for wildflowers and makes the churchyard look extra neat and tidy.

3 **Put up explanatory notices**
Let people know what you are doing whenever you
can – it's a chance to talk about why you want to care
for creation and how your faith is motivating you too.

Put a temporary notice by your meadow area
explaining why it is unmown and when it will be cut.
Pin up your management map in the porch and put it
onto a website, write articles for parish magazines
and speak to the local papers or radio. Always invite
people to share their views, to get involved and to help.

4 **Run an event in Love Your Burial Ground Week**
If you can, please do join in with this national initiative.
Taking place in the second week of June, it is a great
time to show off your lovely churchyard, get together
and celebrate all you've achieved. Use our Education
Pack to encourage children to explore. How about an
activity to create a leaf mobile, or a scavenger hunt
of memorial symbols?

5 **Encourage recording of wildlife**
This can become a compulsive habit so beware!

Put a list of wildlife seen up on notice boards and ask
visitors to make a note of anything that they notice,
encouraging them to make a biological record.
Please try our system for recording, you'll find it
in the **Recording Species** area of our website.
Start with something easy such as a holly tree,
magpie or squirrel. Children love doing this and
it's rewarding for all to see the records of your
churchyard on a national map.

CONCLUSION

Your churchyard can be a haven for wildlife, a place of peace, an ark to open, a treasure trove of local history and potentially the hub of a new community project which pulls people together with a shared sense of purpose and achievement. The churchyard can also be an outward and visible sign of what we believe as Christians – about the value we place in caring for God's creation in recognition of the care God has for us – that we love as we have been loved. The churchyard really is an opportunity and a blessing.

GREAT RESOURCES

Most of the resources mentioned in this chapter can be found on caringforgodsacre.org.uk

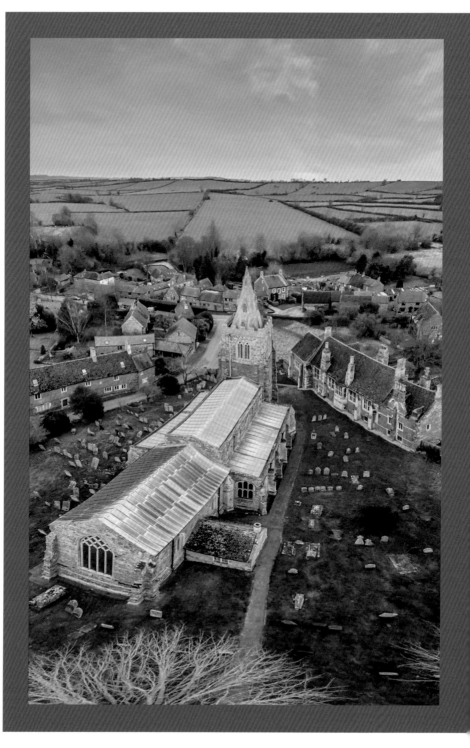

5

BEING THE HEARTBEAT OF A VILLAGE COMMUNITY

——

THREE KEY THINGS YOU'LL LEARN IN THIS CHAPTER

> How your church can affect positive change in village community life.

> How the 'Body of Christ' described by St Paul can be a helpful picture of community engagement.

> Why community audits are important and how your church can lead one.

INTRODUCTION

Anyone who is involved in church life knows that the role the church plays in society is much more than what happens on Sunday mornings. This may seem an obvious thing to say, but even for those of us who know it, in the business of parish life, it is very easy for us to get fixed on the gathered community of the congregation.

The village community can be looked on as a living, breathing body with a number of organs supplying life to it. Every village is different, and the number and type of organisations present in it can vary. Often there are some common features though: the Parish Council, the Scouts or Guides, the village shop, the Village Hall Association, and of course, the Church. All of these connect, normally through shared people and buildings, and as a whole, give the village its character and being.

This concept of people being drawn together by location has been challenged in recent years as we have seen social media become a defining way of drawing online communities together around subjects or particular interests. People were expected to view who they interact with as a choice which has little to do with location.

However, in reality, trends in society have actually placed people much more in their local communities. Working from home, either full or part time, has become normal for many people and workers living in urban areas who can afford to are looking to move to larger spaces with access to the countryside for exercise and recreation.

Social media has been adopted by village communities as a primary way for connecting and organising – sharing news, asking for help and publicising events. Online shopping has taken the emphasis from large out of town supermarkets and opened doors for local producers to sell directly to their communities. The range of functions a village shop can offer has expanded to support this world of online shopping and services becoming a local hub for receiving and accessing these.

Time spent where you live has increased and life lived within the 'body' of the village has become the daily reality for more people.

This chapter will relate to that by looking at the image from St Paul of the Body of Christ and how that is a helpful picture for churches to hold onto in relation to their place in village life. The shape of villages has evolved, and that challenges the health of the body of the community in different ways. However, there are practical steps to help with a village health check through things like community audits and other interventions that can be undertaken or supported by the church.

THE BODY OF CHRIST
IN THE RURAL CONTEXT

The idea of the Church as a body is well known from Paul's letters to the Corinthians in the Bible. In his first letter, Paul describes the nature of that body as being interdependent, with a variety of members who are equally valued (1 Corinthians 12.12-26). In certain contexts, the body of the Church is well-defined in terms of the gathered community that meets together regularly to worship.

In villages, this is not so clear cut, as a much broader spectrum of people would declare they have an interest in the local church.

FOR REFLECTION: Would you term 'the body' as just those who gather on an ordinary Sunday, or would it include those who gather for a Christmas Eve crib service, or those who have gathered there just once, for a funeral?

In this image of the whole body of the village, the church can fulfil the role as its heart. It can be the organ that pumps the life blood through a village and as a vessel of loving service. Indeed, many of the people associated with the church wear several 'hats' and are also volunteering with other organisations locally.

In a village, the church can also be a place where people come, whether regularly or just occasionally, to find refreshment, peace, inspiration and perhaps seeking answers to some of life's biggest questions. This space of sanctuary and sacredness, this nourishment of the soul, affects the health and wellbeing of the whole community, so it's important for the church building and its people to be available in these ways.

CREATING GOOD NEWS 'RIPPLES'

So, if we can see that all people have some sort of connection with the church, whether deep at the core, or further out on the fringe, then what we have is a local pool for natural, effective evangelism – a wonderful opportunity for sharing the Good News of Jesus Christ with the whole of the village. God can work through everyone in ripples of connection and contact that flow from the deep core out, and back again.

Growing the Rural Church in the Diocese of Exeter captures this beautifully in their resource *Lightening the load: freeing the Church for mission* (for more about this resource, see **growingtheruralchurch.org/lighting-the-load**):

'Village communities can act as powerful examples of St Paul's model of the body... Because the community is geographically based, one belongs to the community purely by virtue of living there and all are considered important. There are examples where people whose behaviour is quite unreasonable are still nurtured and generously cared for. Elderly people are automatically looked out for. People with learning difficulties are treated

*with special honour and care. If one is sick, a meal will
appear on the doorstep. People may not be related to each
other by blood, but they have many of the characteristics of
an authentic family who look out for and care for each other.
The Coronavirus crisis has deepened this sense of mutual
care and support for one another in our communities.'*

ISSUES IMPACTING ON VILLAGE HEALTH

It is this sense of community that draws many people
to live in our villages and the perceived quality of life
that goes with it. People choose to invest their largest
financial assets in these places by buying their homes
in villages. While creating huge disparities in wealth and
pushing rural house prices up, this is also a measure
of how attractive many people find these places.
People evidently crave connectedness.

The changing working week

For some, their proximity (in terms of travel time) to urban
centres of employment has been a defining factor in the
choice for people to invest in living in rural locations.
This has created the phenomena of 'dormitory villages'
where during the working week, the village seems
uninhabited and where there is only a limited chance
for commuters to interact with one another and the
community as a whole. However, one of the effects of
the Coronavirus measures has been to force people to
work from home, and one positive outcome of this is that
people have re-discovered the places where they live.

Now that working from home seems here to stay, at least to some extent, it seems unlikely we'll return to how things were. Could the days of the dormitory village be over? If so, this presents a whole new world of opportunities for these communities in discovering a life lived well together.

For some villages though, this investment has not happened, particularly where work that is an easily commutable distance is scarce. For many rural places, the drive has been for younger people to move away in search of better paid employment.

But generally speaking, as working at home becomes much more acceptable, we may be facing a new era for these places as travel time to work becomes less of an issue.

So what does this have to do with the church?

If it is human connection that people crave, could the church be the first to suggest bringing people together? Might it be able to offer spaces for local people to work together? Some people's homes aren't conducive to work, or don't have enough desk space, or facilities like printers etc. A hotdesk away from domestic distractions might be well appreciated, and could be used by business people and students alike.

Local government, environmental and rural development organisations may be looking for ways to sponsor such a project. Take a look at the co-working hub **spithursthub.co.uk**. These kinds of projects invest into the locality and provide reasons for people to stay there. It would also say much about the welcome of the church. Not all projects will turn out to be big building projects, such as the Spithurst Hub. There are lots of ways churches and individuals can make a difference and help boost local facilities:

i) **Bolstering the broadband**

Issues such as low broadband speeds is a perennial problem in many rural locations, and one that the church can have an active part in trying to address. The Church of England has a range of resources to help churches access better broadband and mobile signals for themselves and the whole community (**churchofengland.org/connectivity/solutions**).

ii) **How to mind the gaps**

For some villages, the attractiveness of their geography has prompted many people to buy a second home there, which will go uninhabited for large parts of the year. This can both make these places unaffordable to live in for those who work locally and make community life difficult through lack of continuity and engagement by those who only visit periodically. The body suffers when the regular lifeblood of its people is interrupted in this way. Again, there are interventions communities can consider that look at issues such as appropriate housing and community need through mechanisms such as Neighbourhood Plans. CPRE has more information on this and other helpful resources to support rural places (**cpre.org.uk**).

iii) The power of politics – at its best

Politics is not necessarily a dirty word! Being a parish or district councillor can be a good way of someone living out their Christian vocation with a desire to affect change in a place. Good relations with parish and district councils enable positive change to happen. If you or anyone else is interested in becoming a councillor there is a helpful guide produced by Local Government Association: **local.gov.uk/be-councillor**. There are also lots of helpful resources on the National Association of Local Councils website (**nalc.gov.uk**).

iv) The beauty of buildings

Our buildings and churchyards are also places of opportunity for engaging with our communities. This is something that is often said and often greeted by a sigh from an exhausted Churchwarden or Vicar who has had to raise an inordinate amount of money to keep the roof on a church or has had wranglings over graves. However, it remains the case that for rural communities, and nationally, these places are significant. This is not just because of their heritage value but because they are places that hold meaning for people. It may have been the place where they were baptised, married or buried their parents, but even if not, the fact that this is a place where these life events have happened across generations gives them meaning (see Chapter 2 for more on this).

Our buildings and churchyards are also places of opportunity for engaging with our communities

To borrow a phrase from TS Eliot's poem, *Little Gidding*, they are places "Where prayer has been valid". Churchyards can be havens for wildlife, but also permit visitors to consider some of the big questions in life through their intimate relationship with human mortality – Chapter 4 goes into much more detail about the value of churchyards.

These functions of the building and churchyard go beyond the worshipping congregation and touch on the whole community, which is why they can be excellent places for bringing the community together. They offer a safe space, a sanctuary, for many who feel vulnerable and can be places of reconciliation for communities.

They can host essential services and be meeting places that help tackle isolation and loneliness in a community. For the church community this interaction can build support for keeping the building open and alive with activity. People will feel more confident in investing in a place that is seen to deliver good to the whole community.

There are a number of resources that can help with this. You may want to start with what is published on Churchcare, particularly the sharing your building and finding partners section. There are some great case studies of what can be done creatively with buildings to support communities.

In addition, if you are interested in hosting a community business in your church, then the Plunkett Foundation are offering support with developing projects: **plunkett.co.uk**.

CASE STUDY

Julia is a Parish Nurse in the Two Rivers benefice with 11 churches in Devon. She comes from a background as a Health Visitor and Community Nurse and now volunteers providing 'whole person healthcare' on behalf of the local churches, to people of all ages and of all faiths or none.

Much of her work is supporting people in ways that the stretched local NHS healthcare cannot do, but which mean a lot to those receiving it – being there with time to explain things when people have complex medical needs, accompanying them to hospital appointments and being a safe person to talk to or pray with when someone feels anxious about their health.

Julia links with local health and social care providers, the benefice ministry team and with Parish Nursing Ministries UK in what she does, making the health and wellbeing of the community a key part of the mission of the churches. In setting up a Parish Nursing service, community interest and funds can come from a range of organisations, such as Parish Councils or Lions Clubs, as well as directly from churches. For more information on how to set up a service see: **parishnursing.org.uk**.

COMMUNITY AUDITING

Many churches are very active in their community already and it may be hard to work out what else they could do. I would advocate that periodically churches undertake a community audit to help them in this respect.

Many churches already practice Mission Action Planning and their 'MAP' is intended to set out the vision for the church or benefice in the future and identify some key goals they wish to achieve. The community audit can form an intrinsic part of the MAP process and help you see what opportunities there are for engaging with your community. I'm not adverse to pinching ideas from urban colleagues, so I will highlight this useful guide to undertaking a community audit from the Diocese of London (**london.anglican.org/kb/community-audits**).

i) **Who's there?**

You will need to adapt London's suggested process for your own setting, but it might be useful to challenge yourselves on some of the questions they pose. For example, in the resident's consultation questionnaire given, there is a question on supporting the black, minority and ethnic groups in your community. You may not currently consider your community to be significantly diverse, but how do you know this? Are there Roma, Gypsy and Traveller communities in your area? Are there significant numbers of migrant workers that are housed in your area? What support do they have? How are their voices heard? The Clewer Initiative focuses on the issue of migrants, refugees, homeless people and their vulnerability to modern slavery – see **theclewerinitiative.org**

ii) Healthcare check

In rural settings with the increased centralisation of specialist care facilities and the challenges faced by many local GP surgeries means access to care can be poor. Again, there are practical responses the church can make. The Parish Nursing initiative is one such example where the church can take an active role in supporting the wellbeing of people throughout the community (see the case study on p.91).

iii) Teamwork tips

For some churches, it might feel like the biggest challenge with engaging with the community above and beyond what they are doing already is one of capacity. It is always the same people who undertake most of the work and a sense of exhaustion can set in, particularly if you feel that work is not having the results you'd hope for. For Church of England benefices, working together across the whole benefice can help alleviate some of that. In some places, there may be more than one church in a single village, and

certainly in every place there will be Christians of different denominations. Ecumenical working can bring great benefits, remembering there is more that joins us than separates us in the body of Christ. But what does that working together look like in practice?

One helpful change in the Church of England rules has enabled some benefices to work more collaboratively by delegating powers from individual Parochial Church Councils (PCCs) to a Joint PCC. This does not mean giving up control on all the activities of individual PCCs, but looking at what can be done collectively. It may be the case that building maintenance could be delegated to a joint council, or mission planning can be done jointly, enabling more people who have capacity to join together and support one another in addressing some of these engagement issues.

Details on the changes to the rules and delegating powers to a joint PCC can be found here: **churchofengland.org/more/policy-and-thinking/ church-representation-rules**

CONCLUSION

The aim of this chapter has been to illustrate how village churches can better engage with their communities. The intention is to challenge village churches to look again at this important area, which is about who they are as the Body of Christ in these places. A thriving Church can be the beating heart of a thriving village community.

CASE STUDY

Geoff has lived in the small village community of Lower Beeding, in West Sussex, for over 25 years and during that time has been active with both the church and the Parish Council. He is a Reader and regularly takes services in both the churches in the parish. On the Parish Council he has led the development of a Neighbourhood Plan looking at the community needs in the future in terms of housing and facilities. The church and church room hosts the Parish Council and has hosted exhibitions in support of the Neighbourhood Plan process. During these, hot drinks are provided for councillors and members of the public, making hospitality a central part of meetings.

The Parish Council has supported the church with facilities, including WiFi for the church room where they meet and work together, to support village organisations such as the church, school and village hall.

Geoff's participation in the life of the church and of the Parish Council has been fundamental in building up this relationship and enabling the mutual support which has benefitted the community as a whole.

6

CELEBRATING OUR HERITAGE

—

THREE KEY THINGS YOU'LL LEARN IN THIS CHAPTER

> The heritage of church buildings presents a great opportunity for churches to build relationships with new people.

> Church heritage is both locally embedded and extremely broad – it has something for everyone.

> New technologies are providing new ways to present churches to people who visit and those further afield.

INTRODUCTION

I f you ask a bishop 'what does the word "church" mean?', you will always get the same answer: 'the Church is the people of God', or words to that effect.

If you ask the Oxford English Dictionary the same question, you get a different answer: 'a building where Christians go to attend services, pray, etc.'

For our wider communities – those living and working around parish church buildings – the buildings and the people of the church are inextricably linked, whether "the Church" likes that or not. If we can help those people to understand their part in the ongoing heritage of their local church – the building – it feels like a small step to help them feel like they, too, are a part of the story of that Church – the people.

The same bishop would contend that the Church of England is not a heritage organisation. And yet many of our church buildings are extremely old "heritage" buildings. Around 12,000 of the Church of England's 16,000 or so parish churches are nationally listed for their special architectural and historic interest. The parishes of the Church of England find themselves custodians to nearly half of all the Grade I listed buildings in the country;

that is a great many more than the National Trust, English Heritage and the Historic Houses, combined. The Church of England may not be a heritage organisation, but it has an awful lot of heritage, and that heritage can provide one of the most appealing and enduring links between the institutional Church and the souls of which it legally has the "cure", out in our wider communities.

Since the mid-20th century, many other national institutions, from the NHS, to the education sector, the courts and local government, have sought to shed their heritage buildings – they are judged no longer fit for their modern purposes. But because our parish churches are locally owned and locally managed, Church of England "head office", currently couldn't close them even if it wanted to. Instead, over the same period, we have seen a much more bottom-up approach to church buildings. Local churches meeting local needs, and responding to local opportunities, often in very distinct, local ways.

If we look back in history, we find it was ever thus. Churches are a constant record of the beliefs, enthusiasms and whims of each local community through the ages. If a church building didn't suit current needs, it was changed, and another layer of history came into being. Church buildings are often so old, and have changed so much in the past, that the symbols and scars of change that we see in their fabric today are actually what makes them most fascinating. We can take that thought a stage further: changes that we make to these buildings today are no less a valid part of that record. So, the custodians of our ancient churches really do find themselves in the privileged position of *making history*. This custodianship we have of church buildings is therefore an exciting opportunity for the Church.

WHAT MAKES CHURCHES SPECIAL?

The history we see in churches is rather different to that we see inside other heritage sites, such as stately homes, where so much of what is there is the private record of a wealthy individual or group – a record our ancestors were unlikely to have ever seen. It's a story of them and us. In these places we are guests in someone else's house, looking out for interior design tips and looking forward to a tasty cream tea.

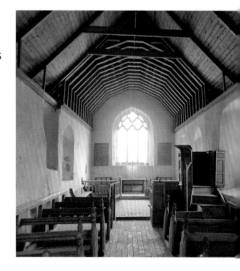

Churches are different. Every inhabitant of this country lives in an ecclesiastical parish, and the majority of these parishes have an old church building as their spiritual HQ. In your parish church you can literally meet your forebears – the people that went before you in that place, walked those streets and lanes before you, perhaps lived in your house; people just like you, but in a different time. You can sit in the pews they sat in where they prayed, sang, let their minds wander, just as we do. You can read the registers where their baptisms, marriages and burials are all recorded for posterity.

Of course, the rich could pay for grand monuments and private pews, but their legal access to the rites and offices of the church were no greater than any other person who lived in the parish, and their stories inevitably ended in the same way, laid to rest in the same consecrated ground; ground which in most parishes is still in use for that purpose today, and where many of us can still expect our own remains to join the communion of bones when our time comes. Understood in these terms, the heritage of churches literally belongs to everyone – there is no "them", only "us".

In his 2003 book *A Christian Theology of Place*, John Inge described historic churches as 'thin places' – places where people can see past worldly barriers to glimpse things about God. He also describes church buildings as 'Palaces of Memory', to reflect their importance in the history of the local community.

The fact that the 'things' of the past exist at all speaks of that God, eternal, unchanging, part of human stories in intimate detail, day by day, week by week, year by year, generation upon generation. It is there in front of us in every artifact; God was there then, is now and forever will be.

And the fact that churches still continue in the same use they have had for centuries gives them a life and a substance that is different to a museum or a preserved heritage building. Being involved with a church is being part of the ongoing history of this country, both religious ceremony and civil society, and a fitting setting for the church's central act of worship, at once communal and commemorative.

There's a recognition of this by anyone who steps into a church who has rarely, or never, done so before, surrounded as they are with echoes of the past, and the stories of Jesus depicted everywhere they look in art and architecture. There's an atmosphere they recognise as different. Sadly, this can often translate to feelings of discomfort, of speaking in hushed tones and tiptoeing about as if this is a place where they don't belong. Reverence and awe are natural responses, but any sense that a church is 'not where I should be' is contrary to everything a church and its people should be communicating to visitors. With warmth, welcome and a generous invitation to listen to the stories in the church's heritage, we can help visitors to feel much more at home in their church.

A NOTE ON CONTESTED HERITAGE: while a church's heritage is for the most part a great blessing to our communities, some objects may be symbols of injustice or sources of pain. This can be an opportunity to learn more about the origins of your community and to respond in the right ways. If you believe there to be something of this nature in your church, see the Church of England guidance and support that is available. Visit **churchofengland.org** and type 'contested heritage' into the search bar.

EXPLAINING CHURCHES ON SITE

The ways in which churches explain this story to their local communities and visitors varies enormously. Getting it right can really help to build ongoing relationships with people, through "friends" groups, volunteering, and through historically-themed events.

Until relatively recently the "church guidebook" was the only tool available to most churches to help explain their building to visitors. Often cheaply produced and poorly illustrated, and always at a cost to the visitor, such guidebooks had limited appeal to the majority of visitors to churches.

Changes in technology and reductions in the cost of high quality printing mean that a glossy, professional-looking guidebook is now within the reach of most churches. But the same technological developments have also brought about wholly new ways of bringing the story of churches alive to visitors, under the general heading of "interpretation". Visitors to museums and art galleries have been familiar for some years with interactive displays, audio guides and themed trails, and all of these technologies and more are now available for churches to use.

The physical kit required for things like audio guides and tablet tours can seem to put them beyond the reach of parish churches. One increasingly popular alternative is the Info Point. This is a standalone device which broadcasts a standard wireless signal which is compatible with the private smartphones and tablets of visitors. This means they can use their own devices to access information about the church. And the church doesn't need to have an internet connection for it to work, and it can even be installed off-grid with solar power.

Using Info Point

As part of a National Heritage Lottery Fund project, St Mary's Church, Frittenden, in Kent, focused on improving accessibility and amenities. This included updating the existing church guides and creating digital versions available for download from an Info Point. Over time, a smartphone tour and other interpretation materials were created by the team of volunteers. Two live webcam streams are also available via the Info Point to indicate to the organist when the bride is arriving at weddings.

CASE STUDY

Info Point at St Andrew's, Castle Combe, Wiltshire

"After months of closure and significant loss of visitor income due to lockdowns and pandemic restrictions, the Government's Culture Recovery Grant scheme, announced in July 2020, appeared to offer us an opportunity to open safely for visitors again.

"Prior to the pandemic, I had learned that Info Point could be used in an unmanned church – visitors could access curated heritage and other relevant information via their smartphones. As part of our plans to reopen, we developed a one-way trail through the church, highlighting items of heritage interest via signage, a visitor assistant and a recyclable paper leaflet. In December 2020, we were delighted to receive funding to develop the trail to provide smartphone accessible heritage information via an Info Point system.

"This has been a substantial joint creative process; from accessing historical records, images and developing content, to a significant amount of digital and computer training for some of us!

"Now our Info Point trail is up and running. Visitors access it by using their phone camera or tablet to scan a QR code on entering the church. Although there is no charge for access, we do ask for a donation if visitors are able to do this. We are very pleased with the feedback to date and are excited to think of future opportunities for developing and using our Info Point system."

Karen Munnings, PCC member at St Andrew's
info-point.com/sectors/places-of-worship

TAILOR YOUR INFORMATION

The information that you choose to tell visitors will depend very much on the individual building. A popular activity to help people explore church buildings is the "church trail". The Arts Society offers assistance in developing an engaging trail for your church. **trails.theartssociety.org**

Whether you are printing a guidebook, compiling an audio guide or designing a trail, you will want to find out as much as you can about the history of your church. Discovering ancient documents in a dusty archive can be as exciting as the church building itself, but chances are your search will begin online. Most county records offices have helpful how-to guides for undertaking research, and archive catalogues are now searchable online. This will help you to make any physical visit to the records office much more efficient and rewarding. **archives.norfolk.gov.uk/help-with-your-research/ the-history-of-your-home/researching-a-parish-church**

If you are concerned that this type of research and writing may be more than you can handle, help is available. The objective in all of this is to help more people learn about the heritage of a church. This is exactly what the National Lottery Heritage Fund wants to support – projects which help more people to learn about heritage. Many churches have been awarded grant funding to help with interpretation in their buildings. A history project a parish church would typically fit into is the NLHF's smallest and simplest grants programme National Lottery Grants for Heritage – £3,000 to £10,000. **heritagefund.org.uk/ funding/national-lottery-grants-heritage-3k-10k**

THE WORLDWIDE WEB

In addition to these new ways of interpreting churches to visitors in person, there is an ever-expanding range of opportunities to do this online.

> All parish churches are provided with a standard template website through the Church of England's **A Church Near You** site, **achurchnearyou.com**. This includes space for explaining the heritage of the church in addition to promoting services and events and giving contact information.

> **Explore Churches explorechurches.org** is another national website which is more focussed specifically on heritage and promoting churches as visitor attractions. Filling in and submitting a straightforward form is all that's needed to give your church's heritage a national presence via this site.

There is strength in numbers, and all churches should make sure they have their pages on A Church Near You and Explore Churches filled in.

That doesn't mean you can't go it alone as well. Some churches share a site with other churches in their benefice, while others have pages on a community website for their village or town. There is a plethora of tools available to help people create a decent website.

One that is currently popular and quite straightforward for the non-technical is **wordpress.com**, or similarly, **squarespace.com**.

DON'T OVERDO IT

––––––––

At this point it is worth a word of warning. Over-interpretation can be very distracting and can even drown out the historic voice of the church it is trying to bring to life. There is no such thing as the definitive narrative of a parish church, so don't try to give this – or if you want to, the expanded edition of the guidebook is the place for it, rather than digital screens in every corner of the church. If you've found out an interesting fact about your church, don't assume you need to laminate it and stick it on the wall. There is something to be said for allowing visitors to "make what they will" of a historic church.

Some visitors, particularly younger visitors, want to use their imagination and discover things for themselves. It is more exciting for them to learn about the mysteries of a church, the things even clever historians still don't understand, and apply their imaginations to them. Whose face is that sculpture? What does that strange graffiti mean? Who planted that yew tree that's older than the church? Historians may be sniffy about myths and legends, but there is no doubt that these engage minds which are bored stiff by a more historically measured approach.

If a building feels exciting, familiar and memorable, there is surely a good chance that that will translate into affection, a sense of belonging and one day, we might hope, a sense of responsibility.

CASE STUDY

Letting people explore and discover

The ruined church at East Somerton in Norfolk is
a challenge to find, hidden away in woodland on the
edge of the village. The formal information presented
at the church is very limited and the ruins are maintained
in a very natural way, with ivy on the walls and a tree
growing in the nave. And yet, this building
is a magnet for visitors walking from the coast,
who value the opportunity to explore and discover
at a mysterious historic site which has not been over-
interpreted. There is something to be learned from
this approach. We should try to interpret these
buildings to visitors, but not in a way that mars that
experience of exploration and discovery.

LEARNING IN CHURCHES

Most churches have historically had some role in local education. Churches are also great places for people of all ages to learn things, about local history, the wider history of this country and the world. Churches can help children learn in unexpected ways: bell-ringing is a form of maths; Gothic windows contain different kinds of geometry; organ pipes are both music and physics; even the stones churches are built from often display interesting fossils and geology. A pioneering example of learning through the church is 'The Queenmaker' escape game designed by History Mystery for Blickling church in Norfolk, which is based around the historical links between the church and the Boleyn family. See **historymystery.games/escape-game-blickling-norfolk**.

CONCLUSION

Bringing a church's many historical stories to life is, at its best, a form of welcome for people of all ages and backgrounds. We can tailor the way we do it, depending on the stories we hold and the people we can most naturally reach in our context. But crucially, bringing heritage to life can convey our human stories as part of God's story and what an amazing, profound thing that is. We may not know how that impacts on individual faith journeys, but it certainly allows us to build relationships with others and remains our opportunity to signpost them along the way, trusting that God will accompany them in the places where we cannot.

7

CULTIVATING FRUITFUL FESTIVALS

THREE KEY THINGS YOU'LL LEARN IN THIS CHAPTER

> With its strong sense of community and its greater awareness of the countryside, the rural church has a unique contribution to bring to its worship.

> When the church gathers for worship, genuine encounters with God can happen, and spirituality, faith and discipleship are nurtured.

> The gospel is Good News, and festivals provide ideal opportunities to celebrate, to be innovative and creative, and to welcome others.

INTRODUCTION

Many people instinctively harbour, or are searching for, some kind of spiritual meaning and connection in their lives, but it may only be vaguely articulated. It's important to provide opportunities to 'tune in' to that where and when we can. We usually find a breadth of church backgrounds represented within a village congregation, but worship is not fundamentally about traditions or styles, texts or music. Worship is about meeting with God.

Every rural community is different, so it is vital to understand context and recognise that no one size fits all. We are looking for 'apt worship' that connects to the heart of a community in language that is readily understood, and which picks up themes which people can relate to.

Churches – like families – tend to have established ways of doing things, often handed down from one generation to another. These are to be treasured and respected, but each new generation brings new innovations and insights. 'Why are we doing this?' is a vital question to keep asking.

When handled creatively, our rich heritage and traditions become stepping stones not mill stones. The rural church has 'good news' to tell and there are many creative ways to do so through festivals, but also through intentionally celebrating everyday faith. It's time to have confidence in God, in the gospel, in the worship, and in the people. This chapter offers some ideas and inspiration to help.

REVIEW AND REFLECT

It can be helpful to spend some time reviewing and reflecting on how your festival services are working. For example, consider:

1 Which festivals are we already doing well?

2 Who usually comes along at key festivals and local celebrations?

3 Where are the natural connections with other groups within the community?

4 What might 'apt worship' look like in this community?

5 How might you renew and resource seasonal worship practically?

Which festivals do we focus on?

Annual festivals broadly fall into three categories:

> **The Christian Year**
>> Advent, Christmas, Epiphany, Lent, Holy Week, Easter, Ascension, Pentecost, Trinity, Remembrance-tide

> **The Agricultural Year**
>> Creationtide, Plough Sunday, Lambing, Rogationtide, Lammas, Harvest

> **Other popular days**
>> Valentine's Day, Mothering Sunday, Father's Day, All Saints' Day/Hallowe'en

Various festivals conveniently punctuate the calendar at regular intervals in an annual cycle. Christmas, Mothering Sunday, Harvest and Remembrance are obvious ones, when church and community naturally come together with wider society to mark the same events. It is worth starting with the most popular festivals and then intentionally building on those, step by step.

FINDING INSPIRATION IN FIVE 'Rs'

1 Renew

At festivals, traditions can run deep with much-loved carols, hymns and familiar readings, but there is scope for refreshing and reshaping to help those not used to church to relate more closely. The nature of a special event readily enables traditional and contemporary elements to sit side by side within a coherent whole in order to connect well with all ages. Here are a couple of simple 'renew' examples:

> During 2020, the Coronavirus pandemic proved that the village church can be enterprising, imaginative, inventive and able to think out of the box. Worship has already been reshaped by going online, so why not

continue to experiment with worship in church too? We are looking for worship that is accessible to all, but rich in meaning. Shorter services with simple, flexible structures are key.

Plough Sunday is important to a farming community, but here, an idealised rural past can collide with present day realities. Theme a service using basic questions relevant to everyone, like 'How do we get our food?' and instead of bringing an antique horse drawn plough into church, why not take the congregation outside to bless the most modern tractor with power-harrow-cum-seed-drill from a local farm?

2 Reclaim

Hallowe'en has gained in popularity in recent years, overtaking Bonfire Night as a main autumn celebration for many families and schools. For Christians, its darker associations are problematic. However, there is an opportunity for the church to redirect its focus and reclaim an earlier emphasis on light, complete with candles and Glow Sticks, linking with known and unknown saints, past and present. Why not include a few interviews of present church members from different generations?

Scripture Union offers free downloadable Light Party resources as a Christian alternative with simple plans for children, youth and all age events. For seasonal outreach packs, see content.scriptureunion.org.uk and click the 'Resources' tab.

Pumpkin carving can be a great all-age activity. For suitable Christian alternatives to scary faces, visit holidappy.com and search 'Christian pumpkin carving'.

In late Spring, we might want to revive a Whit Walk, a tradition stretching back more than two centuries, said to have come about through the Sunday School movement. This celebration, linked to the birthday of the church at Pentecost, can create a focus for churches to come together in a walk of witness full of colour with bright banners and music. The village of Saddleworth on the moors above Manchester continues this tradition, linked to an internationally renowned brass band competition.

3 Rejoice

Summertime sees a fallow patch in terms of the calendar, but this is the season of flower festivals, village fetes and various outdoor opportunities. Some villages have specific worship opportunities, such as services linked to well dressing in Derbyshire; many coastal villages attract holidaymakers and visitors all through the summer season.

St Peter's Church in Walgrave, in rural Northamptonshire, added a Messy Church tent to their regular presence at 'Groove on the Green', which combines a typical village fete with a music festival running late into the evening. Themes of Jesus the Good Shepherd, the Gate, the Way, had clear links with the local countryside and sheep farming within the benefice. Activities included live storytellers, something to make and take away, a collage to create together and display in St Peter's, together with Messy Church merchandise and promotional literature for church services and activities. Other Messy Church events at Christmas and Easter facilitate essential follow-up for baptism as well as fete contacts.

For more information on Messy Church, see messychurch.org.uk.

If you are stuck for ideas, why not offer an Animal or Pet church service over the summer as a way of connecting with local farms, animal lovers and the many pet owners? As patron saint of animals and the environment, St Francis Day liturgies can work well.

Coln Benefice in Gloucestershire has offered a 'Pimms 'n' Hymns' event, and the **Wellington and District Team** has developed informal 'Campfire' worship, which can include building of fires and shelters, and foraging for God. This type of worship celebration lends itself to telling biblical stories alongside local stories.

4 Review

It's worth asking congregations some basic questions about what has worked well over the year, what hasn't, and why? These can then be followed up by more penetrating questions, concerning what might be repeated another year or developed in another season. Annual patterns and repetition help with continuity and allow worship events to become fixed in the minds of local people.

Keep a good record, perhaps on a spreadsheet, of what you did and where for future reference especially in a multi-benefice.

5 Refine

Rural worship should be organic rather than programme-driven, developing out of patient engagement with the community. The use of similar simple structures for different events brings consistency and nurtures familiarity and confidence, and successful events build over time with opportunities to adapt and refine.

That said, a new event can stimulate curiosity and certain buildings offer unusual opportunities. An isolated church with no electricity can be really effective for a Tenebrae Service during Holy Week, in which the darkness and sense of Christ's isolation is heightened.

St Andrew's Church, Old had previously joined in a benefice Remembrance service, but in 2018 they held their own service to commemorate the end of World War I. In 2019, this service was developed further, beginning with the Act of Remembrance outside at the war memorial followed by a procession into the church for a short Memorial Service for loved ones who had recently died. Lunch was offered in the village Community Centre afterwards. The service is already well supported by the village allowing for refining and growth year on year.

St Michael and All Angels, Kirk Michael

Located in the village of Kirk Michael on the west coast of the Isle of Man, St Michael and All Angels is an ancient site dating back before the 12th century. The present congregation is primarily a close-knit family of Christians with a vision statement 'to share the love of Christ with our community'.

'Carols around the Lychgate' involves members of the community and both the Parish and Methodist churches in a 30-minute service. The event is well established, always scheduled on the Monday evening before Christmas, followed by more carols and festive readings in the local sheltered housing accommodation, who then supply the sherry and mince pies.

The Lychgate was originally built in 1907 to house numerous ancient Manx crosses from around the area. The crosses were moved inside the church in the 1970s to protect them further from the weather. The site draws together a rich heritage and an interesting blend of Manx, Celtic and contemporary spirituality on which to build.

In January 2020, the Parish Church led an ecumenical study using the RSCM *Inspiring music in worship* resource. One of the outcomes of these conversations was to review the use of the Lychgate at other times of year. The Lychgate stands alongside a Tourist Trophy (TT) route, the motorbike racing which brings thousands of visitors to the island. The nearby valley, Glen Wyllin, which opens down onto the beach, offers a well-used campsite, so the parish is now considering new ideas for Lychgate, glen and beach during TT season.

Acknowledging the heritage of Kirk Michael, and the enduring interest that many people in the village share in their heritage and culture, another suggestion is to use the Lychgate as a focus on the church's Patronal Festival in September, celebrating both the past and present, the sacred and secular with an accessible blend of traditional and contemporary worship.

KEY ELEMENTS TO BEAR IN MIND WHEN PLANNING FESTIVAL WORSHIP

> - **Venue**
> - **Ownership**
> - **Hospitality**
> - **Participation**

Venue

Some churches are designated Festival Churches, not open for regular weekly worship but available for use on special occasions. Festivals can give these local icons a sense of value and new lease of life. However, it is always worth asking the question: Is a church the best venue for this festival or is there a more appropriate one? Plough Sunday or a Lambing service may work far better in a barn, and an Animal or Pet Service, recreating church with hay bales in a field, enables larger animals to be included.

Brooksby Melton College's Hall Farm is the venue for the annual Lambing Service, with college, farm and church working in partnership. It has proved easier and more practical to take the service to the sheep rather than the sheep to church! Drawing together themes of mothering, new life, Lent and Easter, a short act of worship attracts all ages followed by refreshments and the delight for young and old of seeing newborn lambs, calves and piglets.

We are used to Remembrance outside at the village War Memorial, but there are plenty more options. What about a 'Wild Harvest' or 'Allotment Harvest'? Germinate's 'Rural Mission Sunday' could be celebrated in the local countryside or woodland, and 'Sea Sunday' in the harbour, on the quay or on the beach if you're near one of these.

USEFUL QUESTIONS TO ASK:

> Which location is most appropriate for this festival?

> What will help to create the right kind of worshipful atmosphere?

> How could this event further the mission of the church?

> What is the Plan B for inclement weather if worship will be outdoors? It may simply be 'come dressed appropriately come rain or shine!'

Ownership

Coronavirus has done much to encourage togetherness through joint services online. However, a village community often has a family feel. People may not be able to clearly articulate what they believe about God, but they believe in the local church and consider they belong. Consequently, the idea of going to another village on special occasions may feel like gate-crashing another family party. Don't fight it, use it! At Christmas, everyone wants their own Carol Service in their own church. The whole village tends to turn out with the church full to capacity anyway.

Advent often does not feature outside the church, but there are opportunities to use this creatively. Here are four different ideas:

1 Simply ask everyone to display a sheep or a star in their window to involve the whole community in the build up towards the Carol Service.

2   Until 2018, an annual Beach Hut Advent Calendar ran in Brighton and Hove for eleven years. This idea, which encourages a whole village to get creative together can also be used to help share Christian imagery for all who live locally to see and enjoy. For example, nativity scenes in windows might offer schools, farms, local businesses and residents the opportunity to take part.

3   Latin American 'Posada' sees Mary and Joseph travelling around the village looking for lodging. A simple act of worship with a carol, reading and prayer can be used at each 'lodging', finishing with a Nativity in the village pub on Christmas Eve.

4   Every year, the national Church of England offers resources for a Christmas campaign which achieves an enormous reach. One successful campaign, *#FollowTheStar,* traced the journey of the Wise Men from Christmas Eve to Epiphany with an emphasis on the message of 'God with us', particularly helpful for those who may find Christmas celebrations difficult or lonely. Even though this campaign is no longer running, you could adapt the idea for your own publicity and messaging. For this year's national campaign details, visit churchofengland.org around September time, and search 'Christmas' to join in.

USEFUL QUESTIONS TO ASK:

> Who are our natural partners in the village?

> How can we effectively get other groups and households in the village involved?

> What is appropriate and authentic to our village and our local church?

> How can we foster ongoing engagement through the annual cycle of festivals?

Hospitality

The secret of well-attended and enjoyed festival worship is closely linked to personal invitations and the importance of a warm welcome inside and outside the church.

St Peter and St Paul's Church, Todwick, in South Yorkshire has a gated porch, which for many years had become a repository for out-of-date notices and lost property. After a good tidy up and clean, the porch was transformed into a vibrant, colourful, interactive prayer space with seasonal prayer stations giving a warm welcome to all and providing a haven of refuge and spiritual nourishment even when the church was closed.

Hospitality may be undermined by the timing of services. In a farming community, schedule services at a time when farmers can actually come. And include food! Jesus did a lot of eating and drinking with others and you never come across an unsuccessful village Harvest Supper with local produce!

Hospitality is two-way. A Rogation celebration might begin at church, but as part of the traditional 'beating of the bounds', it could finish with refreshments at a local farm. This involves members of the community who often feel emotionally as well as physically isolated and on the edge.

Lammastide precedes Harvest at the beginning of August. Falling in the summer holidays, an all-age service can include the whole family in baking bread to share together in Holy Communion. This nurtures discipleship in an engaging kinaesthetic way. At Harvest, the local school may add a fresh twist by increasing environmental awareness and responsibility.

> Where is the door already open and where do we need to build bridges into the community?

> How can mutual hospitality be encouraged between church and community?

> Who might feel excluded? The housebound, the isolated or disadvantaged?

> What about the teenagers who frequently get overlooked? What can they offer?

Participation

Carlisle Diocese has developed a 'God for all' slogan, working with the Methodists, United Reformed Church and Salvation Army. These ecumenical partnerships have enabled more effective mission reaching out to remote areas of the Lake District. Rural communities live in a culture where people do not expect to sit passively but get actively involved in village life.

This creates the ideal ground in which to cultivate an integration of worship and community.

It is important to appreciate all people, your non-members as much as your members, building on 'implicit religion', a phrase used by the *Faith in the Countryside* Report (1990). Co-creating worship with the community working together with the church can move 'ownership' onto the next level. It paves the way for plenty of fresh ideas, healthy succession planning, and good, sustainable leadership which is not completely dependent upon clergy, but which values their expertise in taking creative ideas and making them work as worship.

A small rural congregation can feel lacking in both confidence and resources. The local school can be a natural ally. Young people see things differently, offering surprisingly fresh spiritual insights as well as poems, readings, artworks. Music can often be an issue with a shortage of organists in many churches, but a festival may be just the place to enlist the help of a school recorder group or orchestra, or a village choir, or enlist a singing group specially for the occasion which requires no long term commitment.

Now may be the time to rediscover the power of unaccompanied singing. Everyone could learn something new specially for the occasion, helping to overcome generational differences in what people know. Additionally, the Coronavirus pandemic has given us all opportunities to experiment with the use of music in worship without singing, opening up endless creative possibilities.

USEFUL QUESTIONS TO ASK:

> Where are the natural partnerships within the community?

> How might you discover hidden talent within the community?

> How can we share planning to co-create festival worship with others?

> What liturgy and music will span the breadth of age, tradition and style?

CONCLUSION

Focus on one festival. Apply the five 'Rs', revisit key elements to choose a suitable venue, embed ownership within the local community, offer hospitality to every age group, and ensure participation using local talent. Start small and then build on it.

10 TOP TIPS FOR SUCCESSFUL FESTIVALS

1   Nurture a 'can do' mentality with a willingness to learn new material.

2   Form fruitful creative partnerships with schools, businesses and local groups.

3   Celebrate local faith stories alongside the biblical Good News.

4   Be intentional and develop a regular pattern that suits your context.

5   Release lay leadership and celebrate their gifts.

6   Increase ownership and participation by consultation and active involvement.

7   Cultivate inclusivity and accessibility to enable every age group to connect.

8   Develop consistency and continuity to allow things to build and grow.

9   Do a little and do it well to build trust and confidence step by step.

10 Plan and celebrate with enthusiasm. It's infectious!

GREAT RESOURCES

Germinate: Arthur Rank Centre germinate.net – go to Worship Resources. Includes worship resources for the annual 'Rural Mission Sunday'.

Royal School of Church Music rscm.org.uk
> *Instrumental Praise* books – ideal for enlisting a local school orchestra
> 'Lift Up Your Voice' – workshops to encourage congregational singing
> *Inspiring Music in Worship* – a 5-session course of guided conversations to review and inspire worship

Engage Worship engageworship.org –
> Linked with 'Rural Ministries'
> Worship ideas include seasonal prayers, songs, activities, and sketches to engage the whole community, printed and downloadable

Roots rootsontheweb.com Lectionary based all-age materials

Sea Sunday Resources missiontoseafarers.org/sea-sunday for use in coastal areas

Out of the Ark/Same Boat Music outoftheark.co.uk Seasonal music for children for schools; sameboatmusic.com for churches

The Homilies Project lincoln.anglican.org/the-homilies-project Lectionary based, available each week, to enable people to engage with the scriptures without a licensed and theologically trained leader

Chelmsford Agricultural Festivals Pack chelmsford.anglican.org/faith-in-action/rural-issues Resources for Plough Sunday, Rogation, Lammas, Harvest

A good book: *Ploughshares and First Fruits: A Year of Festivals for the Rural Church* by Chris Thorpe, 2020, Canterbury Press

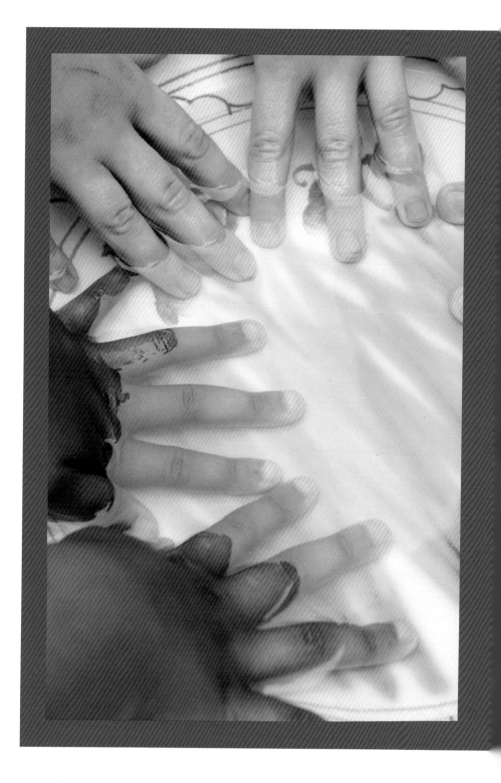

8

WELCOMING MORE CHILDREN

___

THREE KEY THINGS YOU'LL LEARN IN THIS CHAPTER

> Why engaging with younger people is a priority for the Church of England in the 2020s.

> Why village settings can offer great opportunities for creative ministry with children.

> How collaboration with others in the rural community can help boost funding for children's work.

INTRODUCTION

I n July 2020, the Archbishop of York delivered an address to General Synod outlining the three key priorities of the Church of England's vision and strategy for the 2020s.
In it he said:
".....I am enormously excited that, I think for the first time, the Church of England is putting children, young people, schools, families and households at the very heart of its strategy."

In the webinars that followed, which looked more in depth at the theology and outworking of this strategic vision, the Archbishop acknowledged that across the Church of England, our congregations often don't reflect the communities that we serve, and that we long for more diversity, including more children and young people.

Children are often described as 'the future of the church' and that's why we need to invest our time and energy in this area, but anyone in children's ministry will rightly remind us that children have a value and contribution to the body of the Church today.

Children and young people need Jesus' love whatever their age, and as they learn more about what that means in their own lives, they can show that love to others too. Their spirituality and faith can change the world for good just as powerfully as the grown-ups. They can also enjoy and take part in worship just as enthusiastically and can pray just as fervently as any faithful adult. In other words, they are to be an honoured part of the body of the Church, just like every other part.

If there are no children in your congregations, you might wonder where to start in growing a thriving children's ministry, and whether you can sustain it when there is so much else to do.

The good news is that village churches are well-placed to welcome children and support their development, physically, emotionally, educationally and of course, spiritually. This chapter offers some inspiration and ideas to help you do that in a rural context, with ideas for recruiting help from others along the way.

CHILDREN'S MINISTRY IN THE RURAL SETTING

Village settings offer strong opportunities for connecting with children through the Church. These are just some elements of village life you'll recognise and which are an open door for church engagement:

> People know each other and this intimacy means that people readily support each other's efforts. Collaboration between different community groups is common.

> Children often attend small schools, which need visitors in order to offer a broad curriculum, so local volunteers are readily welcomed, creating relationships between local children and adults. Trusted community

volunteers, with appropriate leadership, can offer pre- and after-school opportunities that are vital to parents but beyond the capacity of a tiny school staff, offering strong and stable local relationships.

> Young parents can be supported by small, intimate support groups, which offer a sense of security.

> Church buildings can offer imaginative community space that is both useful, inspiring and welcoming to children and their parents, (see more about this in Chapters 1 and 3).

> There is safe outside space around churches, presenting ready-made learning opportunities, a kind of living Bible, along with connectedness to the land and the providence of God. See Chapter 4 for loads of ideas on this.

> It could be said that the smallest church congregations are often very open to experimentation – there's little to lose and everything to gain from trying out new things that could help welcome more young people and grow the congregation.

> Rural churches have God's glorious great outdoors on their doorstep, which provides plenty of beautiful, open spaces for child-friendly Fresh Expressions like Forest Church and Muddy Church – more about these later.

There can, of course, be challenges too, such as transport links between communities/villages and communicating across a wider region in which there is a multi-parish situation. And in small communities, strong personalities can make or break innovative plans. But these are things which can be managed and needn't be barriers to establishing some simple children's mission projects.

CASE STUDY

Cre8 in West Norfolk

West Dereham is a Fenland village of 450 people with no school, no shop or pub and no bus service. Part of a seven-village benefice, its church has 17 on the electoral roll, mostly over 65. In 2014, led by the Licensed Lay Minister (LLM), they developed a vision: *to support the community in the village by sharing friendship and hospitality and the love of Christ with local families in an informal and non-threatening setting.*

Starting with a children's party, and supported by people from other churches in the benefice, a series of 'Cre8' events emerged, held four or five times a year on Saturday afternoons. Following a promising start, the diocese made a grant of £700. Each Saturday afternoon event follows a standard pattern with a welcome activity, a song, a faith story, creative activity and a simple meal, followed by a special prayer.

The initiative has brought further bookings to the village hall, and developed co-operation in a disparate Fenland community where people do not casually meet and did not know each other. Success has been built by a strong team, clear safeguarding procedures and a good risk assessment, high quality crafts rather than bought-in kits, well-directed helpers who always engage with those attending, and good, consistent publicity. Most bookings come through Facebook, which also has the advantage of recording comments and thanks.

A CHILDREN'S CHAMPION

If you can, finding someone who can lead children's ministry and have a defined responsibility for it is likely to have better outcomes than if it's combined with other ministries.

> Whether this is a volunteer or a paid-for post is down to your context and situation, but bear in mind that the post-holder can be shared across several parishes in a team, bringing village communities (and the children there) together, through the leader's work.

> See what opportunities there are to build on an existing network of relationships. A teaching assistant, lunchtime supervisor, a Brownie or Cub Scout leader, could be invited to help the church, and may later develop a defined church role. A church offering a modest sum to someone to help in a local school can build the relationship between church and school and strengthen ties with families.

> Make the most of the professional advice and support of any regional church Children's Adviser, for example at your diocesan office in the Church of England. They can answer questions, help you in the longer term to develop realistic plans and will direct you to other sources of help.

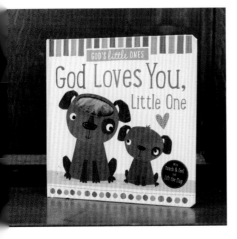

WORKING WITH OTHERS

———

Five ways to seek and find help from others:

1   Always consult with those you seek to serve. Great projects emerge by talking, and talking to the right people means talking in the right places. In the case of children and families, this may not be a PCC meeting!

2   Solutions and projects forged in partnership are always stronger than the ideas of an individual or a closed group. For most rural churches, the local school will already be an integral part of the church's ministry and its contact with local children, so this is a good place to start building on the trust you already have there and enhancing your reputation for good work among youngsters.

3   With the permission of the Head, use that contact with both the children and their parents to find out more about what children in the area need most, and consider how the church can help. Chapter 5 may offer more inspiration for ways to engage and consult with that defined community.

4   Ask neighbouring parish teams about what has helped them, and get someone to come and talk to you about it.

5   Social media, such as the public local community groups on Facebook, are really valuable for inviting comment, ideas and researching plans for children's work too.

CASE STUDY

Faith at Home in Devon

A project in the benefice of Sampford Peverill in Devon, focused on supporting families at home, creating a lending library of 'Faith at Home Bags' to resource parents who have little formal Christian knowledge but express a wish to share faith with their children. The resources are of high quality and are based on either a Bible theme or a season of the church year. The local Mothers' Union and WI groups made the bags, which contain DVDs, CDs, creative prayer ideas, books, games, children's Bibles and candles. Families are encouraged to add things to the bags when they use them. Bags have also been developed for clergy to leave with a family after making a pastoral visit, perhaps to arrange a baptism, a wedding or a funeral. A spin off from this has been the development of a Posada event in the villages before Christmas and the journey of an Easter basket during Lent.

The project was resourced in part by a grant from Scripture Union and required an evaluation at the end of the funding period.

FUNDING AND ADVICE

Finding funding for projects is so much harder when you're working on your own, but partnering with other local children's charities and projects will boost your chances.

> Local and national grants are well worth pursuing. Money from established local charities may be available if a project is suitably devised to meet its objectives, and across a benefice, a co-operative project may find several charities to draw on.

> Bigger charities will require evidence of local investment that they might top up or match-fund; they will always require a thoughtful plan that meets local needs and has realistic goals.

> After researching local needs and resources carefully to create an appropriate project, be bold about promoting it.

> Church donations are often directed towards buildings, so be prepared to talk to people about the value of involvement with young lives and what can be achieved, not just for the church, but the whole community.

> A fund-raising event or campaign will be more successful if contributors can already see a benefit, so ongoing funding may be easier to maintain if you share success enthusiastically.

> The Funding Central website is a mine of information: **fundingcentral.org.uk**. It provides access to information on grant funding opportunities from local, national and international funding sources as well as

social investment from a range of providers. Search the database for funders that match your project. You need a subscription to use Funding Central. It is free for small organisations; £120+VAT p.a. for organisations with an annual income over £100,000.

FESTIVALS

———

Regardless of whether your child-focused projects take place in the church itself or not, you should always extend the widest and warmest possible invitation to children and their families to the big festivals.

Christingle, the Crib/Nativity service, Palm Sunday, Plough Sunday and Remembrance Day are all brilliant times to engage with children, but also their parents, and grandparents.

They will be with their children, so your 'reach' is wider and intergenerational – a wonderful opportunity to welcome them all.

Chapter 7 has lots of great tips on making the most of festivals in rural communities. Just be aware of the language you use during these services – many church terms won't be understood by new families, so use plain, simple, informal, everyday language wherever you can.

CASE STUDY

Forest Church in North Devon

A group of 11 tiny rural churches in North Devon have been experimenting with 'Forest Church'. They have gathered a diverse group of children and adults of all ages, drawn by the spirituality of creation and united by a simple love of being out in the fresh air. There are people of conventional faith and those who would not call themselves religious. Meetings are held in the local woods, and although very fluid in structure, are fundamentally Christocentric and follow the seasons of the year as marked in Celtic Britain. Gatherings attract those who care for the environment and those who want their children to value the countryside. Children of all ages have responded wholeheartedly to this offering. There is no paper; words are remembered or improvised, and songs are chosen that can be readily learnt and remembered. The gatherings have been promoted on both village and church websites.

A GREAT RESOURCE ON CHILDREN'S SPIRITUALITY

The popular book, *Children's Spirituality: what it is and why it matters*, by Rebecca Nye, is an invaluable resource for thinking about children's spirituality and how adults can support it.

In the book's Forward, the Rt Revd Paul Butler, the then Bishop of Southampton, now Bishop of Durham, says:

All human beings are spiritual people. This is the way God has made us. Children are not only no less spiritual than adults, they are often, it appears, more open to their spiritual reality.

The author concurs:

In recent years children's spirituality has become quite a popular topic for research; and a key finding of all these studies is that spirituality is a common, natural feature of most, probably all, children's lives. Certainly no studies have highlighted a type of child who does not possess active spiritual capacities. From a Christian point of view, that makes sense, since it would be difficult to understand why some people would be created without an instinctive capacity to respond to our Creator.

It is easy for adults to get in the way of this, perhaps not recognising the innate spirituality that most children already have.

The book reflects on this in detail, acknowledging that spirituality in general is a hard concept to pin down, but nevertheless is worth considered, careful attention.

Offering practical ways in which adults who work in children's ministry can be spiritually supportive, the author suggests six things that will help children to thrive emotionally and spiritually. The word SPIRIT helps us to remember:

Space

The places where we are can have a positive or negative influence on spiritual well-being.

Process

Recognising that spiritual life is an on-going piece of work. Prayer and worship are spiritual processes, not ends in themselves.

Imagination

How religious imagination can be a powerful tool for going deeper into our tradition and for strengthening our beliefs.

Relationship

Exploring what features of our relationships could help, how are we fed by, and can feed other people's ways of working through things.

Intimacy

Spirituality thrives when there are opportunities to come closer, delve deeper, take risks and pursue passions.

Trust

The author explores how spirituality involves trusting in all kinds of ways, but essentially trusting in God, trusting in the child, and trusting in our faith (the Bible, the liturgy, our doctrines) overall.

If you are committed to children's ministry, this book will be a key resource for exploring these themes, so do consider investing in a copy.

LEARNINGS FROM LOCKDOWNS

———

Despite everything, Coronavirus lockdowns have offered a good deal of learning. Sharing across a benefice has become a more obvious advantage. Instead of travelling everywhere, a leader will have had more space to plan, pray and prepare, and a short online session might in fact reach more participants. YouTube presentations are accessible at any time, enabling families to choose a time convenient to their needs.

> Claire Nichols, of St Mary's Askham in Devon, started *Bears and Prayers* for families in the various toddler groups that she supports, and has found it reaches people in remote situations, even supporting the isolation of first-time mums who might have taken much longer to find and join a baby group.

> Diddy Disciples offers resources for *The Church at Home*, offering a three-section range of options for families to build their own worship.

> **DID YOU KNOW…?** These are great examples of 'mixed ecology' ministry, reaching people in new ways outside of the traditional Sunday church service setting.

CASE STUDY

Special Saturdays near Suffolk

Cheveley is the largest village in a group of four parishes on the border of Cambridgeshire and Suffolk, lying just south of Newmarket, the centre of British horse racing. The villages are surrounded by studs, which, with arable agriculture and the stables in Newmarket, are the main source of employment. These are places where sport matters – a lot. Cheveley church offers a much-appreciated toddler group, Little Angels, run by the parish children's minister, and after a time she consulted with families about the possibility of worship in which they could take part.

Careful consultation revealed that the children do sport on Sundays and on Saturday mornings. But Saturday afternoons, when the racing happens in Newmarket and many dads are busy, is a time when the rest of a family can be at a loose end. So Saturday Special was born. Families gather once a month for a simple act of worship, within which they are fully involved. Themes follow the church year, particularly significant festivals; the gathering, activities and storytelling happen in the nave of the church, and everyone moves to the chancel near the high altar for prayers and dismissal. After this, the toys are brought out and children play as parents enjoy coffee and cake together. A key feature has been that everything offered is for children and their parents to do together: an all-age focus is fundamental.

Through her experience of working with her own children at home during the pandemic lockdown, a parent has offered to take on responsibility for the craft activities.

GREAT RESOURCES

Going for Growth
going4growth.com/home

It's just the Toddler Group
going4growth.com/downloads/Toddler_Booklet.pdf

The Spiritual Child
spiritualchild.co.uk

Godly Play
godlyplay.uk

Forest Church
mysticchrist.co.uk/forest_church

Messy Church
messychurch.org.uk

Diddy Disciples
diddydisciples.org

Bible Reading Fellowship Ideas Hub
ideas.brf.org.uk

Scripture Union
content.scriptureunion.org.uk

Forest School
forestschoolassociation.org/what-is-forest-school

Muddy Church
muddychurch.co.uk

9

REACHING THE ISOLATED AND LONELY

THREE KEY THINGS YOU'LL LEARN IN THIS CHAPTER

> What 'isolation' really means and who is likely to be most affected.

> What the challenges and opportunities are for rural churches to be a part of the solution.

> How to initiate outreach to those most in need.

INTRODUCTION

I t seems that scarcely a week goes by when the local or national media are not expressing concern about isolation or loneliness in our society. Loneliness can have a profound effect on our physical as well as mental health and this has been highlighted by the world's experience of COVID-19.

"The greatest disease in the West today is not TB or leprosy; it is being unwanted, unloved and uncared for. We can cure physical diseases with medicine, but the only cure for loneliness, despair and hopelessness is love. There are many in the world who are dying for a piece of bread, but there are many more dying for a little love."
Mother Teresa

The stigma of loneliness stays a stigma until people begin to open the conversation in an honest and vulnerable way. With all the evidence pointing to loneliness becoming endemic in the UK, one might ask "why is the church not talking about this"?

Perhaps it is that we assume we can never be lonely because we have God or Jesus by our side, or is it that we fear failure in a world which places value on success?

And yet, the Bible makes it clear that we are called to have a special care for the vulnerable, the widow, the stranger and that in doing so, where relationships are formed and nourished, community thrives.

This chapter offers some insights and practical ways of making this a vital part of ministry.

WHAT DO WE MEAN BY 'ISOLATED' AND 'LONELY'?

The terms 'isolation' and 'loneliness' are often used interchangeably, but it is important to recognise that they are distinct concepts, and a good understanding of each is required.

Isolation is defined as 'the absence of social contact' e.g. friends, family, community involvement or access to services. It is therefore a tangible and measurable concept and isolation can often lead to loneliness.

Practical steps can often be taken to address isolation such as improved transport links, increased use of the internet or localisation of services and resources.

Loneliness is a 'subjective, unwelcome feeling of lack or loss of companionship. It happens when we have a mismatch between the quantity and quality of social relationships that we have, and those that we want.'

Remember you can be surrounded by people and still be lonely.

CASE STUDY

Oxenhope Community Café

Oxenhope lies in the heart of Bronte Country and is probably best known for its railway station where The Railway Children was filmed. The Methodist minister Rev David McAloon and the Vicar, Rev Cat Thatcher, both realised that, compared to nearby Howarth, Oxenhope did not have many places where folk could come together apart from the local pubs.

The Methodist Church sits in the heart of the village opposite the local primary school and it was here that they decided to set up a weekly café for a couple of hours in the afternoon, in the hope that it would reach out to the mums and dads waiting at the school gate, as well as locals of all ages. 'We just opened the Church and waited to see what happened!' said David.

A volunteer at the Café talked about its success, "Today for example, we had 24 adults and two toddlers attend with ages through to 90+. It included two people who had not attended before, one of whom has recently been bereaved. People volunteer to help serve, appear spontaneously with home baking, and assist in setting up and tidying away, all amongst the development of new friendships. Looking outward we have been able to donate a small but reasonable sum to three charities – agreed with the guests – which has brought added community spirit to the café."

David and Cat describe the café as more than a place where folk can come and get tea and coffee. Cat said,

"It's a safe environment where people can come and chat and know that they will find someone they can talk to. There are folk who come regularly and those who drop in once a month".

It is also a place that has been beneficial for their ministry. Cat added, "People know that we will be here on a Wednesday afternoon and it's provided a space and opportunity for folk to come and talk if they want to. A volunteer summed up the feeling of the success of the café, "We didn't realise we needed it, until we did it!"

Search 'Oxenhope Community Cafe' on YouTube to see more.

THE LINKS BETWEEN ISOLATION, LONELINESS AND WELLBEING

Social isolation and loneliness impacts on people's health and wellbeing. A report on social relationships and mortality found that living alone and poor social connections are as bad for your health as smoking 15 cigarettes a day and that loneliness is worse for you than obesity (Holt-Lunstad, 2010). Loneliness is likely to increase your risk of death by 29% and lonely people are more likely to suffer from dementia, heart disease and depression. The stigma of loneliness has made it harder for people to talk about it or to own up to it.

The current statistics suggest there are more than 2.2 million people aged 75 and over living alone in Great Britain, an increase of almost a quarter over the past 20 years (Office for National Statistics).

In recent years the UK government has appointed a Minister for Loneliness, and Age UK have put together a loneliness heat map of the UK to demonstrate where in the country people may be more 'at risk' of becoming lonely. Visit ageuk.org.uk and search 'Loneliness maps' to see them.

And loneliness is not just something that happens to older folk. A recent survey by Action for Children found that 43% of 17 – 25-year olds had experienced problems with loneliness. Recent research by Sense has also indicated 50% of all disabled people feel lonely on any given day.

THE RURAL CONTEXT

For many living in rural communities, especially the young and the elderly, maintaining connection can be difficult due to lack of public transport, and fewer opportunities for shopping, accessing public services, employment, and training. These all deepen the effect of loneliness and isolation.

The unavailability of high-speed broadband in rural areas has also led to a growing digital gap between the urban and rural dweller. This digital exclusion was highlighted in 2017 in a study by the Local Government Association (LGA) and Public Health England (PHE) which highlighted the fact that 13 per cent of the adult UK population (6.4 million) had never used the Internet and 18 per cent saying that they do not have Internet access at home.

"Rural social networks are breaking down with a consequent increase in social isolation and loneliness, especially among older people," the report stated.

THE POTENTIAL FOR A CHURCH RESPONSE

It is estimated there are 15,000 rural churches in the UK. Whilst congregations may be small in some, there remains a unique opportunity for your church to respond to issues of social isolation, as often you provide key community facilities and social interaction in rural communities. Here are a few points for reflection:

> Rural loneliness is likely to be exacerbated by physical isolation and difficulty accessing services or leisure facilities. Your church could be one of the few public buildings in the community, so it could be as simple as opening the doors, putting on a kettle, and welcoming people in.

> People in your church may not realise that there are those who may be isolated or lonely in the wider community. But if they did know, most would be only too happy to offer friendship and care. It can be a wonderful way for Christians to express their faith.

One of the surprising things that began to emerge from the pilot of the isolation and loneliness resource at four churches led by the Arthur Rank Centre, was that none of the churches had ever spoken about loneliness or isolation in their PCC. They all knew it existed, they knew there were probably isolated people living nearby, but had never actually talked about loneliness or isolation.

It seemed important that these were conversations that the churches needed to have before they thought of how they might reach out to lonely and isolated people in their own communities.

TIP: If you'd like to raise the issue at a PCC, these discussion questions may help:

1 What does it feel like to be lonely?

2 What makes us lonely?

3 Is being alone the same as being lonely?

4 Do isolation and loneliness go hand in hand?

> Those experiencing the most extreme levels of isolation or loneliness are not likely to be attending community events, church services and activities. Therefore, projects to help reach the most isolated and vulnerable will need to be proactive and have a variety of means to make contact, as well as to gain the trust and confidence of lonely and isolated neighbours.

> Within your church, there may well exist a comprehensive web of networks, which together provide a good starting point to look at your local community. Your members living locally will know a considerable amount about their neighbours and the infrastructure in terms of employment, schools, shops, pub, and social activities.

This knowledge can be discussed, recorded and assessed together, followed by brainstorming ideas that can help.

A HELPFUL RESOURCE TO HELP TACKLE RURAL ISOLATION AND LONELINESS

The Rural Pastoral Support Network Project began in the summer of 2014, following initial research carried out by the Arthur Rank Centre into rural isolation across the UK.

In 2017 the Arthur Rank Centre updated the rural isolation and loneliness resource in response to the national coverage of the subject. It recognised that the Church plays an important role in the life of local communities and as such, is in a unique position to respond to issues of social isolation and loneliness.

Visit arthurrankcentre.org.uk and search for 'Isolation toolkit' to see the resource.

The online resource (paper copies are available by request) goes into detail, but the following section offers a summary of points to help inspire and encourage you to consider isolation and loneliness as a valuable focus for ministry.

The resource takes you through steps for your church and community to consider:

1   **Why address isolation and loneliness?**

Before we rush into action, it's always good to think about who we are as disciples of Jesus, and what church congregations can bring to the issue. What is it that inspires us to get involved?

2   **How do you identify people in need?**

Think about ways in which you can find isolated or lonely people in the community, but also; recognise that some people are quite content to lead what to us may appear isolated and lonely lives. So, these people might prefer befriending in the home rather than joining a group. See linkinglives.uk for more on this. It's important to listen to people talk about their situation, how they feel about it, and respect their wishes.

3   **Ask other agencies**

Even in small communities, there are likely to be some people who represent statutory agencies and authorities: whilst they will be bound by issues of confidentiality, you may be able to set up a referral system whereby they can inform clients of activities you are hosting, and invite them. Examples might be your Local Councillors, PCSOs, GP surgeries and voluntary organisations.

CASE STUDY

Kirkbymoorside Parish

In June 2019, the Parish Church at Kirkbymoorside, Yorkshire, ran a Teddy Bear's Picnic in the grounds of the church. It was a gorgeous sunny day that saw mums, dads, grandparents, and children gather in the church to sing and play parachute games, and to enjoy food and drink outside with more games and fun for all. The event was organised by a retired member of the congregation with a couple of the local mums. "We realised we didn't have very many young families in church and so last year we ran some events around the deanery. They weren't very well attended, so we asked the young mums what they would like and they suggested a Teddy Bears Picnic. It was great to hear somebody say, 'this is exactly what a village community should be doing'. It just felt like it was generous and hospitable and felt that the church was offering something without asking for anything back." This reaching out to families will continue with more events planned throughout the year for children of all ages.

Search 'Kirkbymoorside Parish' on YouTube to see more.

One of the great successes of the Yorkshire Pilot Projects was that the Church was beginning to talk about loneliness and isolation.

HOW TO MAKE A START

1 Safeguarding

For advice and support on safeguarding, contact your church's parish safeguarding officer if you have one, or your regional Church Safeguarding Adviser. There's more information on the national Church of England website too: churchofengland.org/safeguarding

2 Understanding your local area

Carry out some straightforward research to enable you to gain a fuller understanding of local circumstances. Chapter 5 offers some helpful advice on consulting with the local community.

Arthur Rank Centre resource Equipping for Rural Mission has ideas on surveying your community. arthurrankcentre.org.uk

3 Public sources of information

The Church Urban Fund website provides a breakdown of key data relating to poverty in any area. cuf.org.uk

The Office for National Statistics provides information for ward level. ons.gov.uk/help/localstatistics

4 Consultation

Invite people from your community to come to a public open meeting to discuss ideas and agree what could be done together.

5 Publicity

Using local mailings, newsletters and radio are all good ways of communicating events or start-up projects.

Write a press release, approach a local radio station for an interview, do a leaflet drop or send a personal invitation. See Chapter 10 for more guidance on publicity, or ask your regional Church communications advisers for support.

6 Pilot your project

Before launching a new initiative, pilot the idea to assess the way it works, what the demand is and any unintended outcomes. Remember small is beautiful. You may make a difference to just a few lives each year, but every one of them matters to God. Numbers will build over time.

7 Review progress

Carry out regular reviews to assess areas for improvement and to ensure that it is still needed. Send your stories to inspire others through arthurrankcentre.org.uk

PROJECT IDEAS

There are many different groups that can be isolated and lonely. The following is just a snapshot of ideas to get you thinking.

Children

These are all common ways to connect local children and their parents with others:

> Holiday clubs and family fun days

> Toddler groups

> Messy Church messychurch.org.uk and Godly Play godlyplay.uk

Young people

Try these kinds of events to bring local young people together:

> Film nights

> Trips to events in nearby towns

> Funding a detached youth worker

Adults

Research has suggested that older people in care homes are twice as likely to feel lonely as older people living in the community. carehomefriends.org.uk. Visit your nearest care home and see if you can help bring people together there with planned activities, such as:

> Walking/taking residents in wheelchairs through the local area

> Coffee mornings or afternoon tea

Multigenerational events

These are a few ideas to bring people of all ages together for learning and fun.

> **Gardening groups** – children can learn from adults about where our plants and vegetables come from and they love digging in the dirt!

> **Smartphone or tablet digital events** – bring your devices and learn something digital together – make memories by creating digital family photo albums.

> **Lego** – everyone has some Lego lying around unused. Get people together to make and create something amazing.

> **Pottery** – get some air-drying clay and have a 'make and create' session.

Some of these activities lend themselves to discussions around faith too – making crosses, nativity characters or something that depicts a Bible story for example, which can start conversations.

Linking with others

The Church can facilitate activities and be a catalyst for local people to run events such as:

> Hobby clubs

> Befriending projects

EXAMPLE OF IMPACT: A younger woman with disabilities was moved into a rural community and began to attend the church craft group. After a few months she arrived with her birthday cake to share with everyone and said, "this group has saved my life".

CONCLUSION

Rural churches are in the perfect position to make a significant, positive impact on the national issue of isolation and loneliness. The local networks and knowledge within parishes can feed into intentional conversations about the extent of the issue locally and how the Church might help. As well as loving and serving the community by offering care, the relationships that grow from new connections can lead to faith conversations with new people. In short, it is an opportunity for those in need to find friendships, to experience improved wellbeing, to discover the care of God's people and ultimately, God's extraordinary, life-changing love for them.

Rural churches are in the perfect position to make a significant, positive impact on the national issue of isolation and loneliness.

GREAT RESOURCES

Arthur Rank Centre

arthurrankcentre.org.uk

> Read about **further stories** by searching for Issues 77 and 83 of Country Way magazine on the Arthur Rank website.

> Enter 'Research Report' on the Arthur Rank site search to find the **Rural Pastoral Support Network Project Research Report**.

> In addition to the 'Isolation toolkit', the Arthur Rank Centre also offers '**pledge cards**'. They are designed to encourage people to write down what they can personally do in the community to combat isolation and loneliness, and ARC provides a ready-made sheet of the cards in an A4 PDF. The pledge doesn't have to be overwhelming, rather something simple and achievable, such as saying a hello to a neighbour, volunteer, bake a cake, etc.

> ARC also offers '**Table Talk and Puzzling Questions**' – a series of resources produced by the Ugly Duckling Company that can be used to kick-start evangelistically-helpful conversations or discussions in relaxed, small groups. They can be used in the Church or community.

Photo credit: © Johnny Pacner

10

COMMUNICATING EFFECTIVELY

——

THREE KEY THINGS YOU'LL LEARN IN THIS CHAPTER

> How communications can help you reach wider audiences.

> The three key things you must think about before starting any communications.

> How to set up and manage some commonly-used communications channels.

INTRODUCTION

An abundance of apps, digital platforms and gadgets have flooded the communications market in recent years, and many churches have not been slow to realise their potential. Yet with increasing competition for people's time and attention, it's more important than ever that the parish church is switched on to different ways of engaging people which make the best use of time and resources. This can be a real boon in isolated rural communities in particular.

The good news is that with these developments come a range of tools which make communication on a budget easier than ever – and which can help to build strong relationships with individuals and communities for little or no cost.

The steps in this chapter will help you to sharpen up your approach to communications and ensure you don't miss the wood for the trees.

THREE THINGS TO THINK ABOUT FIRST

Before you sit down to plan your communications content, it's a good idea to think about the following three things. This will help keep your communications focused, effective and streamlined.

1 What is your message?

Use your parish vision, strategy and objectives as a blueprint for your communications planning. Even if don't have this yet you could make a list of mission aims and objectives which could be common to many parishes or more specific to you. Here are some examples:

> To be good news to our community, and to share the good news of Jesus Christ.

> Help people of all ages to grow in faith and discipleship.

> Prioritise youth engagement, working with local schools.

> Support the vulnerable and the needy in the community and beyond.

> Pray for our community at local, national and international level.

> Support community events and foster links with organisations, clubs and businesses.

Once you have your own list, next you need to ask...

2 Who are you trying to reach?

It cannot be overstated how important it is to reflect on this question for your communications planning. Too often conversations dive straight into creative assertions: *'we need a video'* – *'we need to be on Twitter'* – *'we need a new website,'* before first asking who these initiatives are trying to reach, and what are the hoped-for outcomes.

Start off by listing as many distinct audiences as possible, thinking about how these relate to your aims.

Include everyone who might have either regular or one-off contact with your building, or any church activity.

Once you have a good list, write down some of the typical points of engagement for that group. If you haven't got one yet, imagine how you might engage.

For example:

> Regular service attendees

> Local people who don't attend services but are open to church and support events

> Users of the church or hall for local clubs and societies

> Parents of pre-school and primary school children

> Local retired people

> People who live alone

> Visiting worshippers (Including for weddings, baptisms and funerals)

> Wedding couples

> Tourists visiting the local area.

3 What is the best medium?

Now you can choose the right means of connecting a message to an audience. This is by combining content (e.g. articles, text, images, graphics, videos) with channels (e.g. magazines, posters, social media posts, website articles.)

Try using the acronym **AME**, which stands for **A**udience, **M**essage, **E**xperience. If your aim is to grow the number of planned givers, then an 'AME' interaction could be:

> regular attendees (Audience)

> watch a video reflection on Christian Stewardship by the vicar (Message) and

> complete a personal giving review (Experience).

You can then measure the number of giving reviews which are completed as a marker of how successful the communication has been.

> TIP: Not every piece of communication will have such a measurable outcome, but by thinking in this way, you will reduce the risk of too much unfocused content which isn't linked to your priorities.

CASE STUDY

A parish church in a popular tourist destination started up a Facebook page, using it to share engaging photos, articles, videos and other content.

The page was successful and soon had over 200 followers, regularly receiving a number of likes and comments.

Examining the page's analytics, something struck the administrators as unusual. There was a particular spike of engagement on a Wednesday evening, as well as very early in the morning and very late at night. They did some asking around and discovered that a lot of the people accessing content at these times were guesthouse owners.

Weekends, especially Sunday mornings, are busy times for guesthouse owners, so the parish decided to think outside the box and start a new service on a Wednesday evening – a less busy part of the week, specifically inviting guesthouse owners to attend.

The service was an immediate success and created an opportunity for those who otherwise were not able to attend services to come into church.

START PLANNING

Once you have those three things nailed down, you can begin to plan. All communications activity falls into one of two categories:

1   Ongoing day-to-day updates to keep in touch with those who are already involved.

2   Special projects, events, appeals and initiatives which you hope will reach a wider audience.

Your day-to-day communication relies on the right platforms to deliver routine information to the regular congregation and those who already take an interest in church life.

If it feels right to segment this into different sub-groups, then do so, but be careful not to spread your regular communications too thinly as multiplication eats time.

Regular communication

The following are among the tools which are good for keeping in touch with these groups;

> Email newsletter

> Printed pew news leaflet

> Text or private messaging services such as WhatsApp

> Local notice boards

> Website articles

> Monthly parish magazine

> Special timely announcements

> Public social media channels

> Closed Facebook groups (where membership must be approved).

Regular communications should be engaging and regularly refreshed. Try to keep a steady and predictable pattern and volume, as this helps to build habit and trust, and encourages everyone to sign up so they don't miss out.

Less regular communication

This might be a one-off event such as a fete, concert or a good news story.

Or it could be a series of communications for a project like setting up a youth initiative, reaching out to a new housing development in the parish, or building links with local businesses.

In both cases, this is where you need to consider tactics beyond the ordinary, including engaging local media.

Finding your voice

Life is much easier if more than one person can compose emails, social posts and web content while speaking with a unified voice. To assist this, you should agree some ground rules for house style.

> Be familiar – use 'we' – e.g. *we're very excited to share news about this year's Lent series…*

> Adopt a friendly, informal, welcoming tone.

> Write assuming no prior knowledge of events or people to be as inclusive as possible.

> Decide on how you will refer to buildings and venues for consistency.

> Illustrate posts with photos of smiling people wherever possible.

Finding skills

It is worth putting the word around to find what skills you have lurking in the parish, be they photographers, web editors, writers or social media gurus. You may even wish to convene a communications group to draw together creative discussions and keep everyone 'on message'.

> **TIP:** Don't limit your search to the church congregation. Seek volunteers as widely as possible across the benefice, ecumenical links, and within the wider community.

'HOW TO' GUIDES

Try these tips on how to set up different methods of communicating. There are some signposts to more detailed 'how to' guides online as well.

Online Worship

Online Worship came into its own during the pandemic, connecting people when physical gathering was limited. Although it's been a steep learning curve to use new technologies for worship and communications generally, many parishes discovered the benefits, including low costs, instant messaging and quick production. Older audiences are getting to grips with it too; keep encouraging them to try out these technologies, as they will help to keep people connected, not just within church, but within society generally.

Ten tips for nifty E-newsletters

1   Try out a free direct mailing platform such as MailChimp, Dotdigital or sendinblue. They often offer good tips once you register and start creating your first mailing.

2   It's usual to send one every week or fortnight.

3   Mid-morning on a Thursday or Friday is a good time for an emailing, so that information and reminders relevant to weekend services can be included.

4   Aim to keep your emails to no more than 6/8 bulletins in total.

5   Make each bulletin as concise as possible – about 150 words each.

6   Include 'more information' links where possible, or an email for a person who can give more information.

7   Start with news from the parish, then further down add links to stories from the diocesan or Church of England news pages, both of which give you ready-made content.

8   E-newsletters with interesting subjects get opened more, so rather than *'This week's newsletter from All Saints,'* call it *'Everything you need to know for Advent'* or *'Don't miss Sunday's pets service'.*

9   Direct mailing platforms allow you to create a 'sign-up' link which can go on the website. You can also email this link to email addresses you already have, inviting people to sign up – this keeps you on the right side of data protection laws.

10 Through instant analytics, you can build a picture of how many people are reading your emails and (if you include 'more information' links), which content they click on.

WhatsApp (or similar) chat groups

WhatsApp, Telegram, Signal and other similar apps allow individual or group chats. They can be downloaded for free from any smartphone's app store. Use the group chat function for discussion involving a number of people where you are encouraging response and multiple input. Expect this to develop a life of its own – but if it becomes a bit overwhelming, you may wish to introduce some informal rules for when it is used and with what sorts of discussion.

> **TIP:** As well as sharing news and information, chat groups are great for prayer chains too.

Social media

While you might look at social media as a single area of activity, what we're really talking about is a variety of channels which each engage audiences in different ways. Here's a quick overview of the main platforms and how they work:

Quick guide to main social media channels

	FACEBOOK (GROUPS)	FACEBOOK (PAGES)	YOUTUBE
HOW IT WORKS	A controlled membership forum where content such as photos, links and announcements can be shared and commented on.	Share photos, videos and articles – either your own or from around the net. Publicly available content.	Video hosting platform.
HOW CAN CHURCHES USE IT?	Keep in touch with existing church members and those in local area. Share news and encourage engagement.	Share content which people are likely to engage with or share to grow the reach and keep up contact between events. Host worship and other online or hybrid events.	Add live and recorded services and events.
TYPICAL AUDIENCE	People who are already engaged with church in some capacity. Be careful of hiding content here that may be of interest to a wider audience.	People you might not know yet. A great way of informally keeping people up to date with what's going on, as well as a hosting platform for live and recorded video.	People who already attend your services, or who might be 'dropping in' to services in other churches.

	INSTAGRAM	TWITTER	WHATSAPP
HOW IT WORKS	Share photos, video and stories. Stylise and annotate images for emphasis. Build into stories.	Share photos and more newsy updates from your church. Engage with a wide number of stakeholders.	Private messaging app
HOW CAN CHURCHES USE IT?	Put colour into what you do. Lift the lid on different parts of church life, and show what is good about your church. Go in detail to different areas.	Engage in wider conversations, current relevant trending topics.	Create smaller groups to keep in regular touch. Share prayer updates, news, requests and administrative information.
TYPICAL AUDIENCE	People you might not know yet. A great way of informally keeping people up to date with what's going on. Instagram audiences tend to be younger than facebook audiences.	Outside your known audience sphere. Twitter is great at engaging with a much wider audience, but for that reason it may not be the place that rural churches need to invest a huge amount of time.	Could be anyone engaged with the church, but ensure you are using it safely, and following safeguarding guidance.

Facebook tips

> Set up a public 'page' for your church. You can share a variety of news, prayer, video and other content. Keep content as relevant to your parish as possible.

> Use to livestream worship and events, encouraging those tuning in digitally to engage within the chat at appropriate moments.

> Make sure you use photos, images and video to make your posts stand out.

> You can also use Facebook to set up a private group in which content can only be seen by those whose membership has been approved.

> Very often villages and rural communities have a local Facebook group which a large number of residents will be members of. This is a great way of sharing posts from the church page with a wider audience – but tailor the content to this group.

DID YOU KNOW...? Because of the way most social media platforms work, if people who follow your page engage by 'liking' or commenting, their contacts who do not already follow your channels will see the content too, so it's a great way to share messages to wider audiences.

Using analytics

Once your social media channels have attracted a few followers, you can quickly access analytic tools showing you who has viewed which posts, and how well each has performed. You will find some content gains more traction than others. Try to learn from this and do more of what works well. You can also use it to understand how your audience behaves, including what time of day they are most active online.

Digital worship

Churches have discovered online worship has the power to reach new audiences. Visit churchofengland.org/resources/church-england-digital-labs for practical tips for how to make a success of this whatever your budget.

Websites

Getting a smart well-functioning website doesn't need much budget or technical know-how. There are a variety of companies, some tailored to churches, which offer combined packages of website hosting, basic design and technical support on a subscription basis. Shop around, but as a guide price a basic website with multiple editor accounts and technical support shouldn't cost more than £250/£300 a year.

> TIP: Every church also has an automatic listing on achurchnearyou.com which now allows the addition of pages and content – and may well be all you need. This is absolutely free.

See churchofengland.org/resources/digital-labs/blogs/ten-top-tips-when-writing-web for some excellent tips on how to write well for your church website.

Getting a smart well-functioning website doesn't need much budget or technical know-how.

Photography

Whether printed or digital, the right photo can bring your messaging alive in ways text alone cannot achieve.

Advances in digital photography mean that even with a smartphone it is possible to capture most of what you are likely to need.

Many rural churches are beautiful and in stunning locations, and images in all seasons should definitely be on your list. These are easy to arrange and less likely to require special permissions.

Ensure you also get photos of people, events, services and what makes your church buzz, so you can give newcomers a sense of what they could come and be part of.

> **TIP:** Run a competition for photos of your church building. This is a good way to identify skilled photographers locally, and will furnish you with a bank of images.

Print

Print still has its place, especially for those in the community not connected to the internet, or if your area has poor broadband and/or mobile 'not spots'. Noticeboards/ad spaces at local shops, pubs and schools can also be great places to share information.

Parish magazines

There are broadly two kinds of parish magazine:

1 The kind run by the church and distributed chiefly to those who feel an attachment to the church.

2 The kind which is run independently.

If it's the latter, hopefully the church has the opportunity to add news and reflections, but if not, this is worth establishing. Either way, these are a vital resource for those who either are not online, or who still prefer their news and information in printed form.

Rather than catch-all articles, tailor different content to different audience groups within your village, particularly if it is delivered to every house.

Posters/leaflets

If there are notice boards at the church or elsewhere in the village, use them. Keep information up-to-date, and use posters with bold simple information and a website address for detailed information.

Create a simple welcome leaflet so that these can be placed in the church for visitors to take away, particularly for those who visit the church when nobody else is present.

The signage, notices and information encountered by those visiting the building should not assume prior knowledge and start with a broad welcome. See Chapter 1 for more on this.

Working with local media

When you want to reach a wider or different audience to those who regularly engage with church you will sometimes need to work a bit harder than just your own channels. Whether it be an event you are hosting, or something that has happened which can help to tell a positive story about faith and the church, the local media should be on your radar.

Media liaison

Stories from rural churches can be of great interest to local news outlets, with their remit to cover a broad section of local community life.

Use the support of your regional (diocesan) church communications adviser. They can offer tips on media relations, making your story stand out, photography and how to write an effective press release. There are some great tips on cofeguildford.org.uk – type 'How to write a press release' in the Search.

Broadcast media

If a TV or Radio news programme is going to cover a story, they will want to know what elements can make up a short feature. This will always involve short interviews as well as establishing material such as shots of an activity in progress or recordings taken at an event with lots of people present – it's worth thinking about what these might be before you contact them.

Again, contact your regional church communications adviser for support with interview and filming opportunities and how to manage them.

Safe and legal

It's important to make sure that communications risks are considered and policies put in place to protect everyone involved. Everything that would be true for safeguarding in church is true online, so see this as a positive way of modelling good practice.

Some important starting points are mentioned below, but there is lots more information on the Church of England website: churchofengland.org/safeguarding

> All parishes should include a safeguarding message on its website front page. This should say that there is a safeguarding policy – link to it if possible, and give contacts, both in the parish and at diocesan level for anyone with a concern.

> Anyone who manages your social media accounts should have seen and signed the parish safeguarding policy. You should also discuss social media protocols including what to do if disclosures or concerned messages are received via social media.

> Care must be taken when contacting under 18s or anyone who may be vulnerable. If you have any doubts as to age, make sure to obtain parental consent.

Check the policy and practice guidance of the Church of England's website for a range of resources to help make this task straightforward, including model consent forms and more do's and don'ts on digital communication.

Data protection

There is a range of guidance online for parishes to make sure this is covered, (see churchofengland.org/gdpr for some useful pages), and if there is somebody locally who is prepared to act as the information controller and check everything is compliant, then bite their hand off!

Photo permission

It's important to obtain specific photo permissions for shots where one or just a few people are shown and identities are clearly visible. For group shots, you can announce at the beginning of an event that photography will be taking place, and nominate seats or a certain area which people can move to if they do not wish to be photographed.

DID YOU KNOW...?

Under GDPR you shouldn't store photos on a personal device. Photos taken on a phone or private camera need to be moved to a GDPR compliant storage facility in the name of the Parish, and then deleted from the private device.

Evaluate, review and renew

Is what you are doing effective? Try to make time at least once a year to review your communications. Focus on developing what is working well, and consider cutting back or changing anything which isn't always aligning to audiences and ensure you are reaching the groups identified. Remember – a lot of Facebook 'likes' doesn't necessarily mean your comms is being successful in what you want it to do, so make sure you measure your efforts against your vision and strategy aims.

Ask for feedback at events which includes questions about how people heard about it.

The Church of England's 'Digital Labs' Learning website has lots of tips and suggestions for how to improve communications which are up to speed with all the latest platforms. This is a free resource and can sign up for their free webinars and courses at churchofengland.org/digital-labs

CONCLUSION

Focused communication will support your parish vision and strategy and ensure that all your efforts are efficient and have more chance of being effective. You can cast your net wider with the support of professional colleagues and speak of the Good News in countless ways to countless people. Some communications tools can help combat isolation too.

AFTERWORD
BY THE ARCHBISHOP OF YORK

___

From cultivating fruitful festivals to children's spirituality to how to make the best of your churchyard, this timely and helpful book about how village churches can thrive has been full of practical advice and encouragement.

There is much I found exciting in this book, but it was particularly encouraging to discover how the rural church uses technology to develop its mission as well as making use of all the COVID-19 pandemic has taught us. For at the heart of the Church's witness is the constant desire to share the good news of Jesus Christ and to make him known in all our communities.

And, of course, we are all aware that learning to live compassionately and justly with the Earth of which we are a part is the greatest challenge facing the human race – and this is yet another area where the rural church takes the lead.

If you live in the country, you know that growth happens in due season. You know that a tree in winter is no less healthy than a tree in spring. You know that things bear fruit at the appointed time. And you know that if you want things to grow then you must pay attention to the roots. So having now read the book I hope you will have found it to be a new gardening manual for the village church.

My hope and prayer is that it will not only be of practical benefit to thousands of rural churches in England, but also restore confidence that the village parish church continues to have a viable future and occupies a vital place in the whole ecosystem of the Church of England.

✠ STEPHEN EBOR: